AF332982

# I am built inside you

# Contents

# Preface

*Contemporary And (C&)* is an art magazine and a dynamic space for the reflection on and linking together of ideas, discourses, and information on contemporary art practice from diverse African perspectives. *C&* was launched in 2013 and has since attracted a great deal of international attention with its weekly features, columns, reviews, interviews, workshops, and events, on the continent and in the Diaspora.

*C&* provides a space for major players, young cultural producers, and artistic discourses from international African perspectives—on the web and on the ground: apart from the online platform, *C&* has produced six very successful print issues since 2014 and has presented them in Dakar, Bamako, Kampala, Lagos, Venice, New York City, and São Paulo, among other places.

The idea behind starting an art magazine such as *C&* was the ambition and essential need to create a networking platform for artists, curators, critics, and academics—from Johannesburg to Cairo, from Lagos to Oslo. *C&* has succeeded in visibly bringing together the extreme diversity of artistic practice in Africa and the Diaspora. This idea was preceded both by a study commissioned by ifa on (re)presentations of contemporary art in Africa and the Diaspora in the German context and the comprehensive ifa project "Prêt-à partager," a transdisciplinary artistic platform on art, fashion, and urbanity, which was first presented in several African cities with exhibitions, workshops, and events before coming to Germany.

From the beginning, *C&* saw its mission in providing information to a readership interested in the arts—on the African continent as well as in Europe, the Americas, and beyond—on the tremendously diverse and progressive art practice in Africa and the Diaspora. One of *C&*'s key concepts consists of making art scenes—the art scenes of this world that have so far been ignored by the Western-dominated canon and art market—accessible to an international audience ranging from artists to art experts and art lovers.

I am pleased that after *C&*'s first successful years, we have been able to compile a publication with a selection of the most defining contributions to the magazine, thus presenting to a wider audience a repertory of the significant content *C&* has generated in the past four years.

—Elke aus dem Moore
Head of the Visual Arts Department at ifa

# Editors' Note

Since its launch four years ago, *Contemporary And (C&)* has not only called attention to exhibitions, artists, and curators from African perspectives through a vast number of texts by international authors, but has also circulated new, persuasive debates. Long before the supposed "hype" around "global art," *C&* generated discourses that are only slowly coming into view in other international art media.

Beyond our online archive and our newspaper-format print issues, we have now decided to build another library of selected *C&* content: a *C&* book series featuring a sampling of significant texts and interviews that have broken new ground and played a crucial role in shaping the canon of contemporary art. Following a new thematic structure, the book interrogates major issues such as postcolonialism, globalization, and migration from parallel perspectives, issues that are also receiving greater attention in the Euro-American art world.

The present publication marks the beginning of the series. *I Am Built Inside You* is a compilation of eighteen pieces published by *C&* in the past four years. The book's point of departure is a conversation with the great South African artist Helen Sebidi, which was published in September 2016 in *C&*'s print issue #6, released at the thirty-second São Paulo Biennale. The artist, curator and educator Gabi Ngcobo had invited Helen Sebidi to participate in the biennial. We compiled a volume with other significant pieces from the *C&* archive that expand upon and contextualize Helen Sebidi's concepts, perceptions, and reflections from diverse perspectives.

The following collection comprises conversations and several essays reflecting Sebidi's very distinct viewpoints on topics such as home, tradition, history, and spirituality: from the curatorial visions of Thelma Golden, the pioneering director of the Studio Museum in Harlem, to the activism of the artist collectives Village Unhu (in Zimbabwe) and lugar a dudas and Afroexistencia (both in Colombia). Also featured are conversations with the legendary artist Senga Nengudi about the ritual and philosophy of her complex performances and with the emerging Tabita Rezaire from Johannesburg, who in her practice calls herself a "warrior-healer." We also showcase theoretical perspectives, such as an essay on the major writings of historian, anthropologist, physicist, and politician Cheikh Anta Diop about African identity and a conversation with renowned scholar Walter Mignolo on his concept of decolonial aesthetics/aesthesis.

The texts are interspersed with quotes, moments of disruption. By way of association, these voices reflect an approach within our practice: taking nothing for granted but repeatedly pausing to contemplate, allowing space for other perspectives, and modifying our own.

—Contemporary And (C&)

We decided to settle
into individualism, and
even the sand used to
make the bricks is sand
that comes from this
land.

Mame-Diarra Niang, artist

# Rural Hope after a Bitter Harvest

*A conversation between Helen Sebidi, Gabi Ngcobo,
Luciane Ramos-Silva, and Thiago de Paula Souza
Tuesday, September 6, 2016*

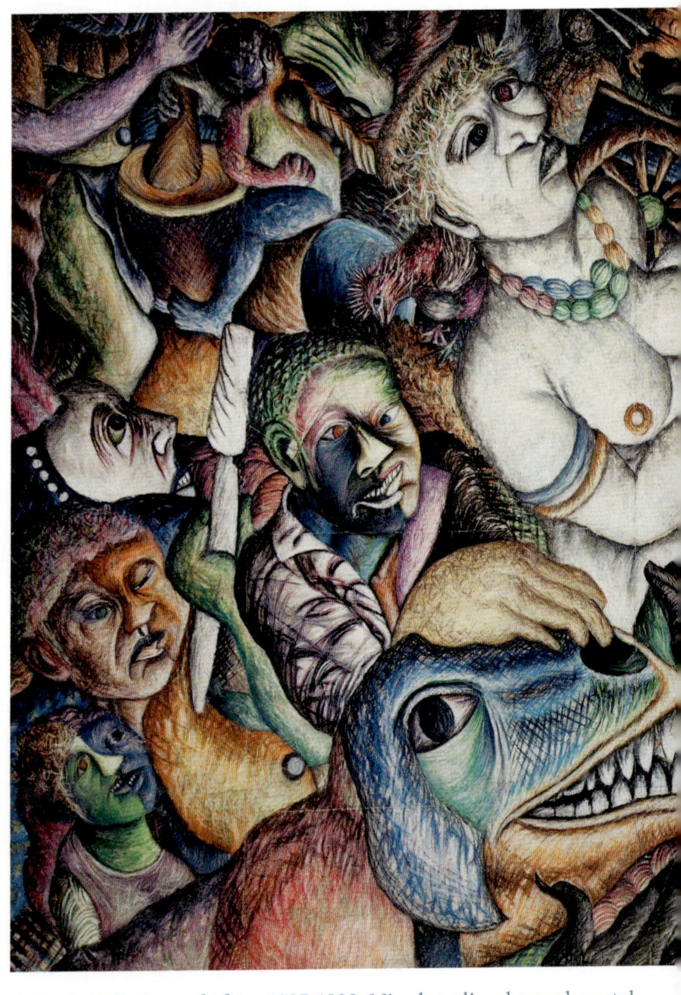

Helen Sebidi, *Tears of Africa*, 1987–1988. Mixed media, charcoal, pastel on paper. Courtesy of the artist

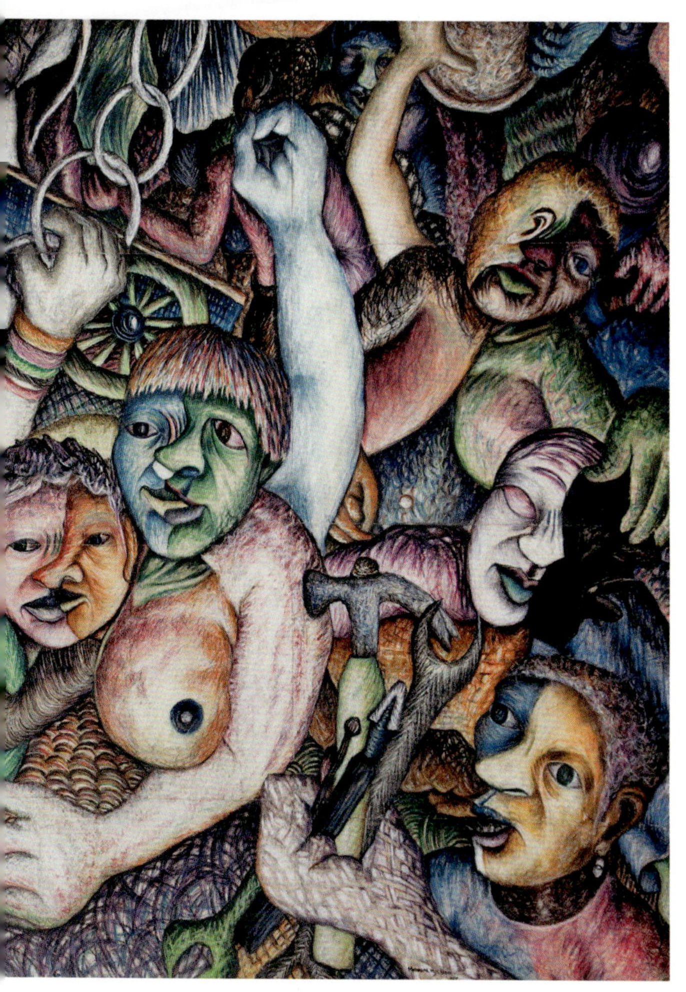

*Luciane Ramos-Silva:* Could you introduce yourself, bringing in the idea of home as a place where we can be, a place we can belong, and home as your place of art?

*Helen Sebidi:* Home is my place of art. I believe that charity begins at home. Traditionally this was a moving home, not a home to own like we do now. You have to be natured in your home. I also need to communicate with other homes; that is my duty. Other homes means that you are building the human being inside, alone, and the being is held spiritually by those who help you to see the world. Those people will also say to you, "We don't own this world; we are its messengers." We have been given the task of a messenger to transform culture and to communicate. My grandmother used to say to me, "I am built inside you." It is therefore my duty to move this world as well.

*Luciane Ramos-Silva:* Thinking about land and country, tradition, community, could you elaborate on those spaces you came from? Because in Brazil we don't have so much connection with the histories and realities of South Africa, so could you tell us about it?

*Helen Sebidi:* I would start with the land. Our people were working on the land in order to follow the path that the Creator had given them. Then the European community introduced pensions, but our people said: "We don't want to be given money from those people. These people want to take our land that was given to us by the Creator to do work for Him." They rejected the pension because they believed that what they had been born for is what they have to work for. So traditionally I would say, the seeds were planted by the Creator and when the reward comes, we have got it here in our hand, we worked for it. We must know our seed and that is the only way that we will save growing cultures, communicating cultures. Before that happens, we will suffer. Africa was the first continent that was built and made by God, by reality. The Creator knew what He was doing. I am proof of who I am and I still say, I will never ever join someone else's culture without communicating. My grandmother died in 1981. She pointed at me with a big finger and told me, "You are not going to work for white people. Your parents have been taken by white people, but you are not gonna be taken." As I travel around, I take with me all the seeds she planted in me.

*Gabi Ngcobo:* I would like to take a cue from your description of Africa and the complexities of Africa as a continent in order to speak about the work you will show at the 32nd Bienal de São Paulo, *Tears of Africa* from 1989, which you created before the car accident you were involved in in August 1989 ...

*Helen Sebidi:* ... even before my understanding of the continent. During the conflicts in the townships

of Johannesburg, I happened to see death. I happened
to have blood all over my clothes when a child was
shot. I had gone away from the Johannesburg Art
Foundation and moved to Alexandra (a township) to
teach, and the same things happened there. I was
shocked. The people who came from Europe brought
their culture to our continent. They stopped those
who came from the rural areas because they knew
they would come and demolish the town. And when
you went to the rural area as a township person,
you used to be stopped and told not to come back.

*Gabi Ngcobo:* Stopped by whom?

*Helen Sebidi:* Stopped by the white people. We
had to report at the police station to be allowed
to sleep in the township, otherwise we were arrested.
You would go for six months, then, when you came
back you were caught and went to jail because
you crossed the border against the law. It was a pro-
tective measure that was helping them to keep
our people working for them. That is a kind of slavery
that made our people much more severely dominated
because they left their work and when they were
supposed to pray they had to pray to white people,
even today. So of course we made them richer and
richer.

*Gabi Ngcobo:* What do you think about showing
*Tears of Africa* in Brazil? What do you hope for the
people seeing this work?

I've seen artists in a good mood when they painted, but the final results are still some- how gloomy. You know, it comes from inside. It comes from indivi- dual suffering, and that's reflected on the canvas.

Sam Nhlengethwa, artist

*Helen Sebidi:* The people who see this work could think of how to help our people return to praying in the same way we learned at home. They could find their way back because their ancestors were shipped to Brazil as slaves, not knowing where they were going. So now they will have to get back to learning how they can pick up the seeds. Their freedom will come when they pick up the seeds.

*Gabi Ngcobo:* When you say they can find their way back, do you mean this symbolically, through your work?

*Helen Sebidi:* I think they will learn who they are and live who they are and be sure of who they are— in Brazil. Those tears of the ancestors will change, it will be love, it will not be tears anymore but it will be something that will help communication, and the chains of the tears will disappear. Because they will have their own seeds and they will know where they are going and what to do.

*Thiago de Paula Souza:* You will produce a new work for the biennale, which will be shown together with *Tears of Africa*. I am interested in how you have been developing your work over the years: your skills, your techniques, your way of producing your art in the context of the new generations you have witnessed being born and growing. Could you also talk about the differences in generational spirit,

17

especially because some younger people may think of themselves as so-called "born frees"?

*Helen Sebidi:* I don't think there is any such thing as a born-free person. Because born-free people don't understand—that is why I have spoken about ownership—that we don't own ourselves. We need to move around and see things properly, knowing that we don't own anything. When you don't go to the other side you don't see what is there. It is like my work. I don't know what I will be doing when I reach the studio in Salvador, Bahia. I will be surprised by what I bring back after visiting all the places I go to. My dreams are partly important for my production. But I also just start by playing and following what comes from in here and from out there. In the end, that is where I am able to guide what I have been doing. It is spiritually awakening and I am quite happy be able to work that way.

*Luciane Ramos-Silva:* To get back to *Tears of Africa*, it evokes a sense of people seduced by the life of the city, right? I am thinking about your transition and your experience in Johannesburg and outside of South Africa. Could you talk about those bridges?

*Helen Sebidi:* There is a big gap between the rural areas and the city in South Africa. City life developed by stealing from the countryside: white people stole the skills of the rural population and claimed them as theirs. If there had not been apartheid in South Africa, the rural areas would have been well developed and the world would have understood that Africa has the best forests.

Gabi Ngcobo is curator of the 10th Berlin Biennale (2018). She was one of the co-curators of the 32nd Bienal de São Paulo in 2016. An artist, independent curator, and educator, Ngcobo is a member of faculty at the Wits University School of Arts in Johannesburg.

Luciane Ramos-Silva is an anthropologist, choreographer, and community arts organizer. A doctoral candidate in performing arts, she is a member of the editorial advisory board of the magazine *O Menelick 2°Ato*.

Thiago de Paula Souza lives in São Paulo, where his current research for his master thesis concerns race relations, African and Afro-Brazilian art, and the depiction of art from Africa and the Diaspora in the German-speaking context. He formerly worked as an educator at the Afro-Brazilian Museum (Museu Afro Brazil).

# If Truth Was a Woman

*A conversation between Euridice Kala and Aïcha Diallo*
*Thursday, May 5, 2016*

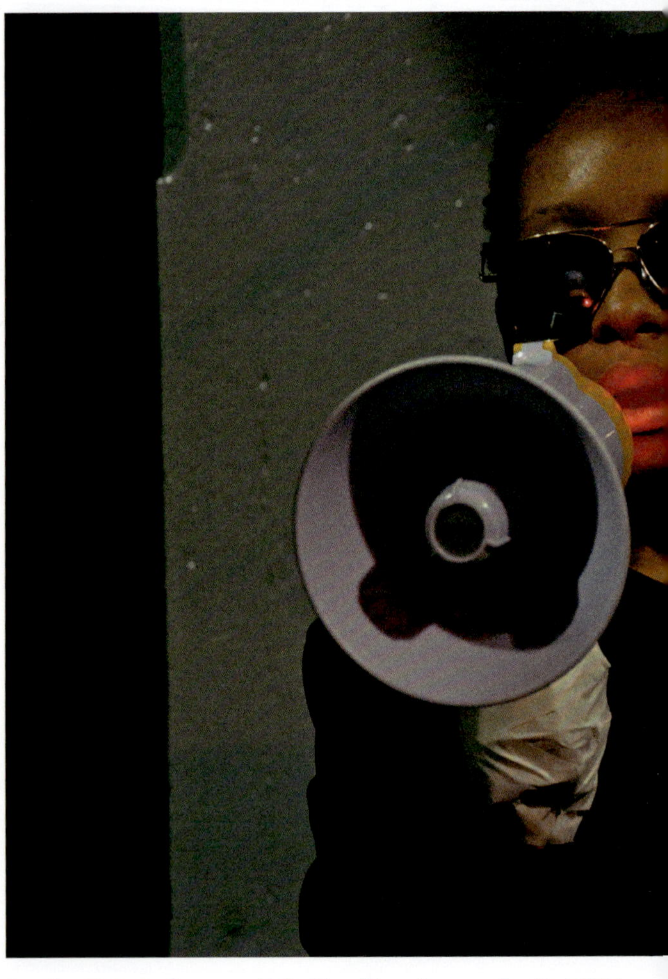

Euridice Kala, Performance *Tedet Time (From Compound to City)*, 2014.
Public Acts, Johannesburg. Photo: Akona Kenqu

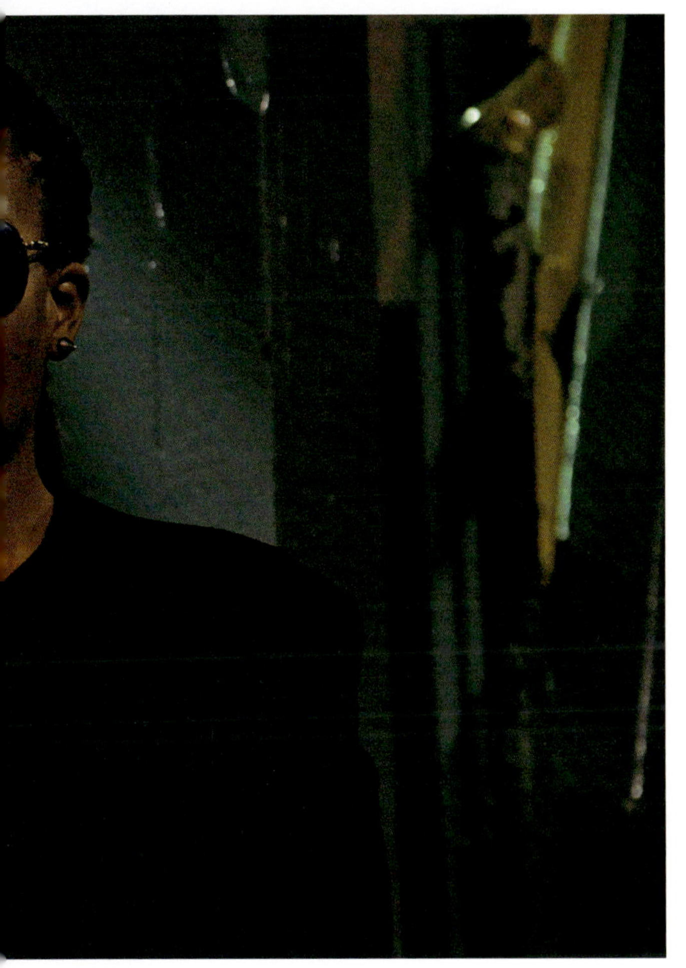

*Aïcha Diallo:* What were the artistic influences that you experienced growing up?

*Euridice Kala:* My childhood was a training ground for what I do now. Although my mother Ana Arrone was not an artist herself, she exposed me to art. She would bring me books to read, musicians to listen to—she was a reference for the tastes I developed in music and for my visual preferences. She would talk about how young people were feeding their thirst for culture, music, and art in the early days of independence in Mozambique. We listened to Bob Marley, Kool and the Gang, Freddy Mercury, Prince, and many others. She was able to provide me with an entire world to which I would escape whenever the real world became too rough or too stale. And this entry into a transcultural space and language has influenced the manner in which I am approaching life. Although she passed away in my late teenage years, she was able to instill an insatiable curiosity in me. She was magic …

*Aïcha Diallo:* Your work *Will See You in December … Tomorrow (WSYDT)* portrays a conversation with your grandfather about his memories of colonial Mozambique. What was that like for you? And what kind of stories do you want to tell through the different media you use—from photography to video to performance?

*Euridice Kala:* My relationship with my grand-
dad (Armando Arrone) is one that has remained
with me over the years. We were always friends and
shared football matches and time in his carpenter's
workshop experimenting with wood, while he
would tell stories of colonial Mozambique. I am a
proxy war child, born during a period that was very
challenging for all Mozambicans. Maputo was
crowded by UN workers and the country was on
the brink of democracy. I have inherited a city and
a country that were formed without considering
people like me. Our constitution and laws took a
long time to develop—such as the legality of same-
sex relationships, which was only revised in 2015;
the rape laws that decriminalize the perpetrator if
he marries the victim; or, last but not least, the late
developments in family law that, until very recently,
were governed by the Catholic Church. Outdated
laws passed during the colonial era still pervade
my experience as a Mozambican living today and
give me insight into colonial times. *WSYDT* mirrors
these connections with our colonial history and
explores what has been unconsciously appropriated or adopted into our national constructs.

In an interview, Samora Machel (the first presi-
dent of independent Mozambique) was asked if he
thought the liberation movement and political

party Frelimo had acted too soon. His response was that it had moved when the opportunity presented itself, but I think Frelimo's ideals were lost after independence. As a result, we don't have a strong sense of identity, and perhaps this is why there is little involvement in arts and culture. Also, making Portuguese the official language reduced the possibility of diversity in many institutionalized contexts, resulting in bureaucracy and demagogy.

*WSYDT* foregrounds different narratives—for example, connections with the East dating back to the eleventh and twelfth centuries, when traders from India and Indonesia brought fabric (capulana), spices, etc. Our appropriation of Portuguese and a broadly Western academic context have become our only apparent connection with the rest of the world. My piece is about questioning these colonial influences.

The stories I tell challenge the archive of this Western canon—they seek to intervene and expand this archive in order to form new connections with our present lives.

*Aïcha Diallo:* As well as working as an artist you are also a curator and researcher, for instance for the platform PAN!C. What's your perspective on cultural collaborations and networks?

*Euridice Kala:* Art making is difficult anywhere, and especially so on the African continent. My first instinct is to be an artist and to be as carefree as possible; however, when you are a young Black woman from Africa (excepting perhaps South Africa and Nigeria) it is really, really hard. In Mozambique, we don't have structures to support artists. For this reason I moved to South Africa, where I accepted a position at the Visual Arts Network of South Africa (VANSA).

Here I have established various programs such as PAN!C, which aim to stimulate art production and its circulation across the continent. For instance, the Boda Boda Lounge—a video art festival—has been instrumental in creating platforms that are inclusive. I have learned that through sharing and participation, diversity happens. I am really weary of a homogeneous representation of Africa and African culture—of a superficial oneness defined by the use of a certain fabric (capulana) for fashion trends, natural hair, or afrobeat, etc.

Capulana fabric, for example, is not originally from the continent but represents early intercultural exchanges. Music styles vary greatly from Cairo to Cape Town, ranging from avant-gardists such as Luka Mukavel (from Mozambique) to movements such as Pungwe. Through the networks that we have been able to create, cultural circulation and exchange can take place.

*Aïcha Diallo:* You consider yourself a feminist. How does this stance inform your artistic practice?

I and some other
Kenyan artists were left
in shock at such a
global form of contem-
porary art. (We may
have been regarded as
ignorant of the shock
factor in contemporary
art, however.)

Donald Maingi, art historian

*Euridice Kala:* I am a feminist now; more specifically, I am a Black feminist from the African continent. What I mean is that feminism in Maputo may differ slightly from other contexts. For example, women here who don't shave are not doing it as a challenge to patriarchy; it's simply a cultural thing. Forty percent of the Mozambican parliament is made up of women from various parties and cultures, but that does not translate to the inclusion of women in positions of power in the various sectors. My feminism is about challenging conditions under which the lives of Mozambican women have had little to impact across the board.

*Aïcha Diallo:* What are you exploring at this year's Dak'Art?

*Euridice Kala:* My installation *Supõe Se a Verdade Fosse Uma Mulher_ E Porque Não?* (Imagine If Truth Was a Woman—And Why Not?) makes connections between slavery and later colonial times, with the presence of elements such as the white wedding dress and a white wall. It challenges constructs of whiteness, such as the idea of purity, by creating a chart with various resources from the continent that are all white—ivory, cotton, powder.

It approaches the present time and looks at African struggle fighters—the construction of the sole hero—and the possibilities that the archive should include other partners by featuring their spouses' names in a conversation more open to other additions and manners in which to author our histories.

Aïcha Diallo is associate editor and coordinator of *C&*. Of Guinean heritage, born and raised in Berlin, Diallo is a cultural producer and educationist with a focus on migration, empowerment, and communication. She graduated in European Studies at Queen Mary, University of London (B.A.) and in Intercultural Education at Freie Universität, Berlin (M.A.). She worked for the cultural platform Chimurenga in Cape Town, the exhibition project prêt-à-partager at the ifa – Institut für Auslandsbeziehungen, as editor of the online publication focusing on cultural productions and spaces published by the Heinrich Böll Stiftung, and as co-founder and actor of the performance platform Label Noir. In addition, Diallo is a program co-director of Kontext Schule at the Institute of Art in Context at the University of the Arts, Berlin.

# Directing a Museum That Responds to History

*A conversation between Thelma Golden and C&*
*Tuesday, May 12, 2015*

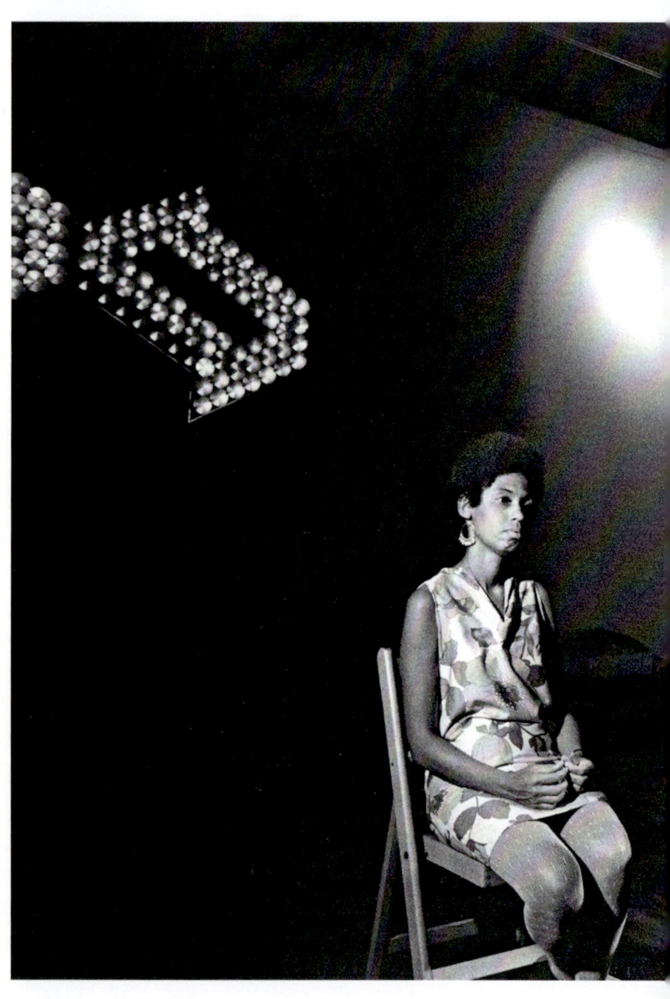

At the Studio Museum's 1968 exhibition, "Tom Lloyd: Electronic Refractions II." Courtesy of the Studio Museum, Harlem

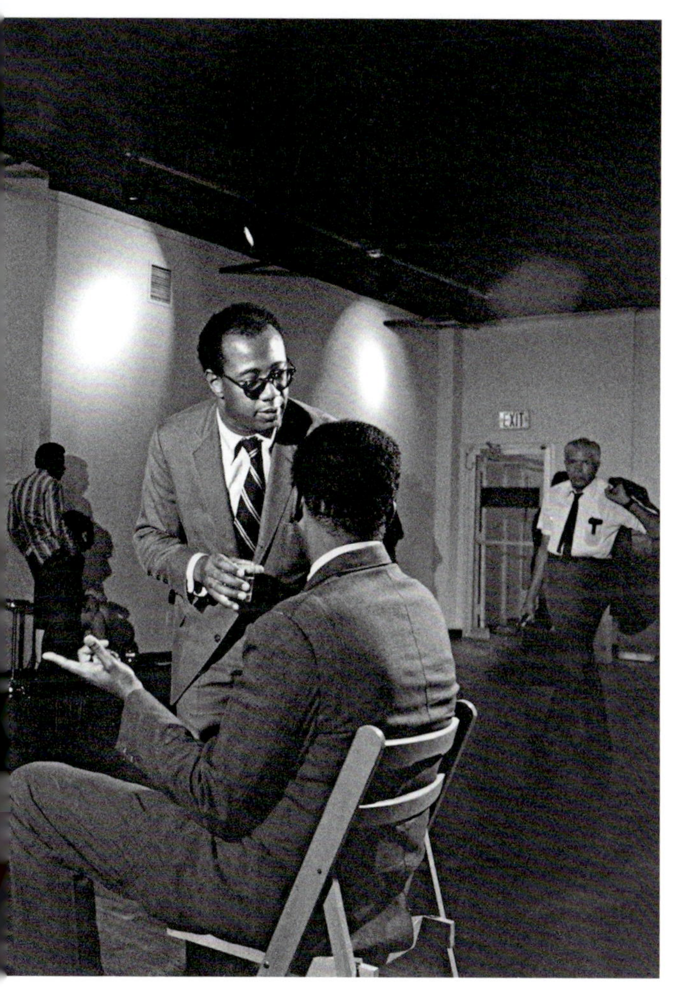

*C&:* Since 2000, you have been the director and chief curator at the Studio Museum in Harlem. How did you start this journey?

*Thelma Golden:* My relationship with the Studio Museum began back in 1985. I had an amazing opportunity during my second year at Smith College to work with the curatorial department and the museum's director at that time, Dr. Mary Schmidt Campbell. Dr. Campbell is a pioneering cultural visionary, arts leader, and art historian. So that internship with her really set out the building blocks for my career in the art-museum world. When I graduated from college in 1987, I worked as a curatorial assistant at the Studio Museum for a year before working at the Whitney Museum. When I came back to the Studio Museum in 2000, I had already worked at the museum twice for two different directors, Dr. Campbell and Kinshasha Holman Conwill. I came back as deputy director and chief curator at the invitation of the new director, Dr. Lowery Stokes Sims, and I succeeded Dr. Sims as director in 2006.

*C&:* The Studio Museum was founded in 1968, in the midst of the American Civil Rights Movement. What was the museum's role during that time?

*Thelma Golden:* I have had the wonderful opportunity to spend time with people who were involved in the Studio Museum's founding—people who were in the conversation before the doors even opened, who envisioned the museum and then did the work to make it happen. The idea of the Studio Museum went hand in hand with many other ideas and projects of that moment. When I talk to people, many of them artists, who were involved with this museum in the early years, they say they saw themselves as creating not only a museum that would collect and present art, but an institution that would have a singular role in the development of a community.

*C&:* How has the museum's structure and vision grown and changed since then?

*Thelma Golden:* I think what is so amazing and interesting about the Studio Museum is that it always changed or responded to different moments in the world of art and culture. This is an incredible testament to the different women who have led it during my history here. This museum has beautifully risen to each moment's dialogue—sometimes leading it, sometimes responding to it, often doing both at the same time. When I was here in the late 1980s, Dr. Campbell made an extremely powerful argument for a revisionist art history, a rewriting of a mainstream story that had simply excluded the contributions of artists of African descent, as well as Latino artists, Asian artists, women, and many others. I am truly proud that this institution continues to help rewrite history by creating exhibitions that fill in these missing pieces of history in any number of ways.

C&: What is the Studio Museum's current role as a social space in reference to the very tense circumstances of Ferguson, the Eric Garner case, etc.?

*Thelma Golden:* I think an institution should provide a framework for conversation. The experience of art, the inspiration and the instigation that art provokes, can serve as a way for people to understand themselves and the world. At the Studio Museum, we have amazing programs for young people, including really innovative high school programs, which have art making at their heart, but also use art making as a way into storytelling and conversation. So at the moment when young people are discovering themselves and considering their place in this world, art can provide the ability to articulate and develop their voices in very powerful ways—especially when tumultuous event are happening in the world around us.

C&: Let's talk about the rapid spread of the term "global art." Suddenly every museum wants not to only focus on Jeff Koons and Ed Atkins, but on non-Western art perspectives as well. Why is an institution such as the Studio Museum even more important right now?

*Thelma Golden:* I am not sure this issue is an either/or. I think that the opportunity to have artists

of African descent showing everywhere is fantastic.
I think it is also important to have platforms that
exist to present the specificity of artists of African
descent. I really argue for both and all of it.

*C&:* The Studio Museum's permanent collection
includes around two thousand works. Can you tell us
a bit more about your collecting approach behind it?

*Thelma Golden:* Our permanent collection
embraces all media and ranges from the 19th century
to the present. We have a broad approach to
collecting, as we seek to really represent and tell
the stories of the incredibly broad range of artists
of African descent. But in the collection we also
explore and manifest very specific ideas and experiences. For example, the Studio Museum takes its
name from our foundational artist-in-residence
program. Every year we have three artists working
in studios here in the museum, and they have an
exhibition at the end of the year. We acquire work
by these artists—so the collection is a marker of
the many artists who have worked here and become
part of our community as part of this program.
Of course, we also collect artwork from our exhibitions. "Freestyle" (2001) was the first of what has
become a kind of signature group show, nicknamed
the "F shows," when we feature a dynamic group
of emerging artists. It was followed by "Frequency"
(2005), "Flow" (2008), and "Fore" (2012). We acquired

work from all of those exhibitions, and many others, so the collection also reflects our unique exhibition history.

*C&:* 2018 will be the museum's 50th anniversary.

*Thelma Golden:* Yes! We're incredibly excited and have a number of projects and programs in the works. One really important project that we're trying to do is to capture the stories of the many people who have been intimately involved with the museum since its founding—the many directors that have been involved here, the curators, the artists who've been in our exhibitions, and our many, many trustees, donors, members, and supporters. Secondly, we are thinking about a project that really analyzes these fifty years in the reception, collection, and curation of artists of African descent. Finally, we are beginning to put together a project that we are calling "inHarlem," taken from the name of the Studio Museum in Harlem. It's a series of site-specific public projects in the neighborhood. For our anniversary, we would like to create projects that not only reflect on the neighborhood, but also exist as a vital part of it.

# Reclaiming African Culture from Western Ethnology

*By Gabriele Genge*
*Tuesday, June 28, 2016*

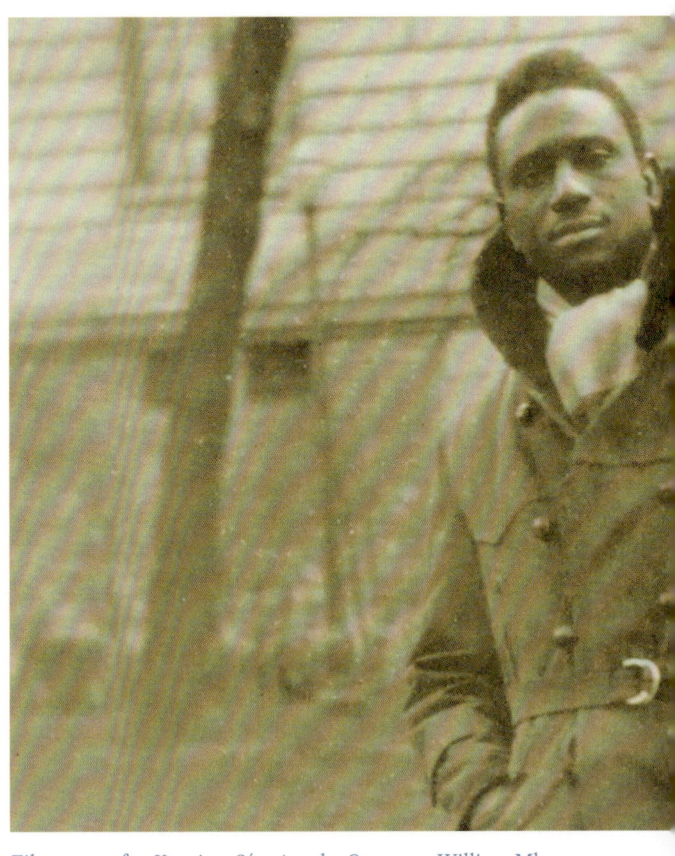

Film poster for *Kemtiyu–Séex Anta* by Ousmane William Mbaye

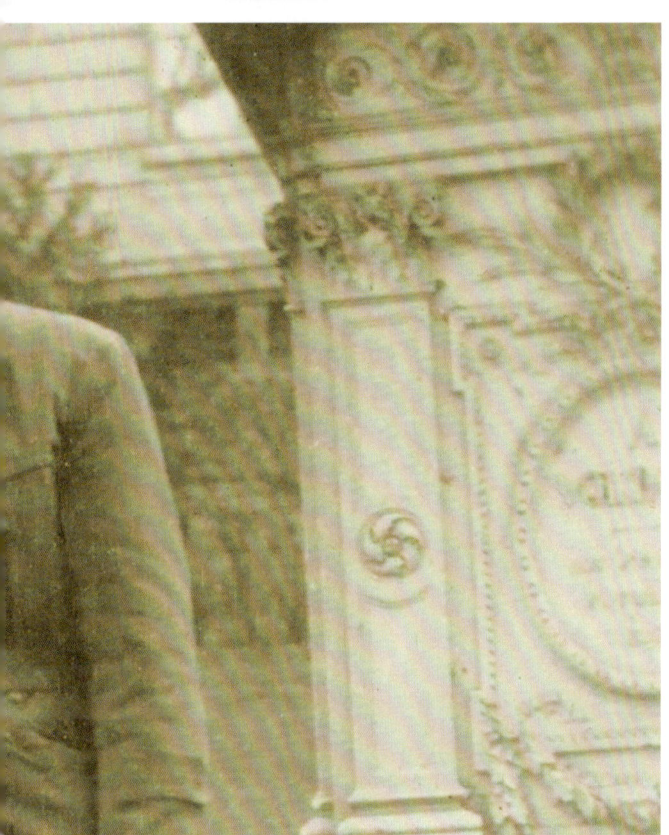

In 1948 Cheikh Anta Diop, still a student in Paris,
wrote an article for the Parisian magazine *Le Musée
Vivant* exploring, for the first time, an idea that he
would continue to pursue in his later academic and
political career: the concept of nationally unifying
Africa under the umbrella of a uniquely African cultural heritage. Later, as one of the most radical African
intellectuals, he considered the depressing status
of African art and culture under French colonial rule.
He further put forward that he could imagine "con-
structing the humanities on an Egyptian basis for
reasons of the geographical and historical order—
in the same way Greek is the basis of the humanities
in Western civilization."

Diop would follow up these statements with great
enthusiasm in the coming years, replacing the colonial
concept of African animist or Bantu philosophy, for
instance, in vogue since 1947, with strictly scientific
evidence of the totemist Egyptian tradition in African
culture, thus building a new nationalist concept of
Africa. The epistemological standing of Diop and his
concepts of totemism that I would like to elaborate
here is multilayered and difficult to encapsulate.
When he began his academic career in the 1950s, his
studies at the Sorbonne, the École pratique des
Hautes Études, and the Collège de France were widely
interdisciplinary, moving between nuclear physics,
Egyptology, and linguistics but always focusing on

his unitarian project of decolonizing the African humanities, deconstructing the Western claim on civilization, and universalizing cultural hegemony. Methodologically, his ideological project sought to separate African culture from Western ethnology and to secure a tradition that—lacking ultimate documentation—could hitherto only be fixed in a repertoire of images and linguistic catalogues, doing so using the anthropological and historical methods of his time. He wished to prove the anteriority of an African-Egyptian "race" by examining anthropological bones and comparing physiognomy, reviewing linguistics, and, last but not least, elaborating a concept of totemism, which to this day has not drawn any scholarly attention whatsoever.

Diop's tremendous project of birthing a complete, brand-new construction of national heritage relying on images is therefore of great interest to art history. Furthermore, we are confronted with a radical destabilization of the Western resources of cultural heritage, which were paradoxically deconstructed as ideological devices by an intellectual who nevertheless positioned himself in the midst of a traditional Western "order of things," to quote Mudimbe.

As early as 1954, Cheikh Anta Diop insisted on the concept of totemism in a brief paragraph of his dissertation. And it is the aesthetic concept of an alien relationship between the apparently confounded

realms of nature and human society that seems to
have affected him more and more, even to the point of
delivering iconographic proof for his comparative
and yet unprovable argument of a historical and contemporary African-Egyptian totemism.

To conclude, Diop's meanderings among the sub-
strata of totemistic construction could be interpreted
as an effort to denounce a Western epistemological
tradition of dividing nature and culture by displaying
pictorial forms, instead seeking to trace migratory
traditions as evident testimonies of a long-lasting
cultural heritage. For Diop, a far-reaching political
object was at stake, and he seems to have returned to
his research interests in totemistic heritage only when
it became clear that his political career in Senegal
had to come to an end. He was excluded from high
office as an overly eccentric and radical representative
of an African stance in the humanities but later
lent his name to the University of Dakar, which is now
called Université Cheikh Anta Diop.

Diop's deconstruction of Western legitimacies
provokes a fundamental change in the humanities
that, as Kobena Mercer puts it, "is relevant to all
aspects of art at a time when globalization is intensifying
transnational flows of peoples and cultures."

Gabriele Genge is professor of Modern Art History and Theory at the
University of Duisburg-Essen, Germany.

# Photos of a Time When Spirituality Was Fluid and Inchoate

*By Olufemi Terry*
*Tuesday, July 8, 2014*

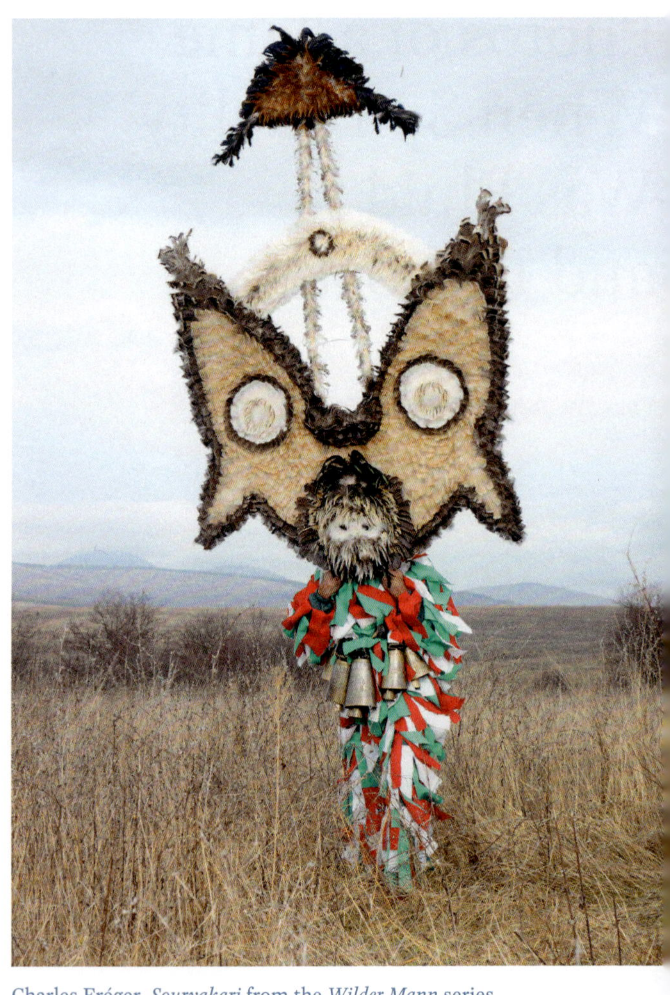

Charles Fréger, *Sourvakari* from the *Wilder Mann* series,
2010–2011_0057. Courtesy of the artist

45

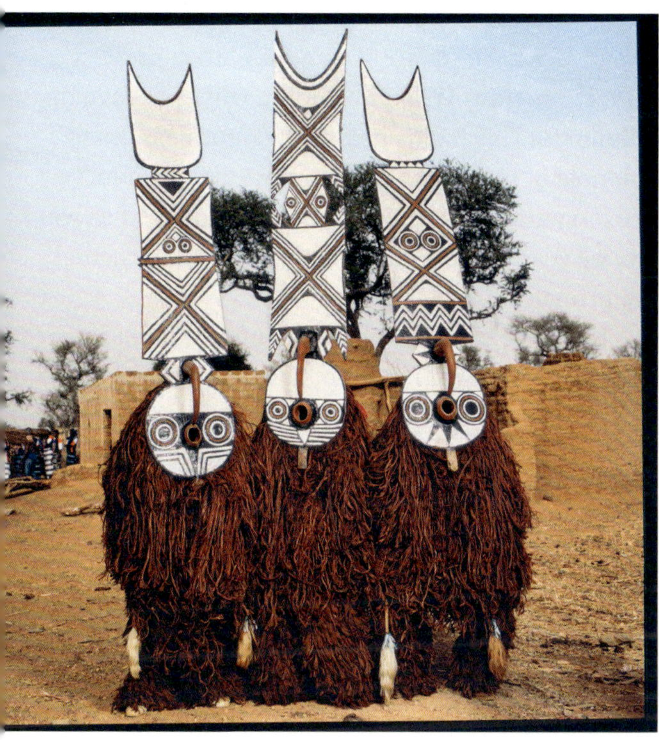

Phyllis Galembo, *Bwa Plank Masks*, Yenou Village, Burkina Faso, 2006. Courtesy of the artist

In the foreword to photographer Charles Freger's *Wilder Mann: The Image of the Savage*, Irish novelist Robert McLiam Wilson wonders why "we gave up religion for this." This being "the depthless grand guignole of mass media idiocracy." "Plugged in," Wilson writes, "neurotically wi-fied and G3d as we are, we yearn to re-establish contact with the actual, the primal, the old."

Evidence of a wide revival of interest in masquerades and folk traditions can be found in several recently published coffee-table books aimed at the art and design scene: *Wilder Mann*, Axel Hoedt's *Once a Year*, and *Maske* by Phyllis Galembo, a survey of masquerades that occur even today in Haiti and across sub-Saharan Africa.

Europe and Africa lie on more or less opposite sides of Wilson's "this," yet there are startling, unambiguous parallels between the images and motifs in *Maske* and *Wilder Mann* respectively. This is unsurprising. Europe's pre-Christian past is not dead, only deeply buried.

For the non-Westerner, it is tempting to satirize that continent's efforts to reconnect with its pagan roots by training on Europeans the sort of exoticizing anthropological gaze so often directed toward African and Asian customs. This has already been done. But it is also intriguing to note the subtle distinctions that set Europe's revived masquerades apart from their African counterparts.

In *Wilder Mann* costumes, I perceive what I'll call a post-modern animism, an animism concerned equally with conservation as with depictions of the material and spiritual worlds. Many of *Wilder Mann's* masqueraders appear, perhaps unconsciously— and in some sense after the fact—to be critiquing modernity and its attendant environmental degradation. The pastoral settings of the *Wilder Mann* portraits and the vivid animality of the costumes represent nature; but they also glorify it, setting it in unambiguous contrast to the contemporary world of industrialization, gadgets, and convenience. But that opposition is framed in a visual vocabulary largely derived from monotheism's stark dichotomies: good/evil, Black/white, rich/poor, spiritual/material.

By contrast, in the African masks of *Maske,* one perceives more disinterested and unitary representations. In the polytheistic beliefs of the Yoruba, or even those of the ancient Greeks, the gods were capricious and demanded appeasement, and there were a great many spirits (mischievous, even malicious ones). Life was filled with mishaps and unpredictability, but there was neither god nor a devil.

Of course, in one sense, African masquerades, like the *Wilder Mann* costumes, are ceremonies that signal engagement with and resistance to the pressures of conforming with the homogenizing influence of globalization. But the African masks evoke an older milieu that has not lost all its power, and in this context, they stand in opposition to nothing; they merely depict and signify.

With its title denoting a lycanthrope—the offspring of a bear and a woman—*Wilder Mann* conjures the atavism and primitivism of a time when human spirituality was fluid and inchoate. But *Wilder Mann* references also man's duality, his brutishness, which has been an indispensable asset in building civilization.

Even as the outlines of fading cosmologies are evident in Freger's portraits, the full complexity of European paganism appears elided and greatly simplified in his work, perhaps in the service of marketing. Freger alludes to the goat, the bear and the devil in addition to the *Wilder Mann* himself. It is not difficult to guess the symbolism of each of these figures, or that they may have been chosen from among many historic archetypes for the reason of their transparent symbolism.

The goat represents the home, domestication, and even advancement of a sort, for he is the companion that proves his usefulness by sacrificing meat, milk and wool.

The bear stands for the wild beast that can be mastered or subdued but never absolutely tamed; the bear is of value, chained and dancing, as uneasy evidence of man's power over the natural world, over dumb beasts. Yet the bear is the ancestor too of the *Wilder Mann* and shares the same fraught (even Oedipal) relation with him that mythic Prometheus had with Zeus: the forebear eclipsed and then persecuted by his descendant.

Alone of the four *Wilder Mann* archetypes, the devil approaches the ambiguity and fluidity of African masquerade spirits. He is described in Freger's text as "the intercessor between the world of the living and the dead who, paradoxically, generates more laughter than fear." Although the Christian Lucifer has been superimposed onto this primeval devil, traces of his original persona and attributes persist in the character of the medieval fool or jester.

In the foreword to *Maske*, Chika Okeke-Agulu wonders "why … does masking persist in such vibrant form in parts of Africa and its diaspora … despite the threats posed by the combined, if antithetical, forces of secularization, fundamentalist Christianity, and radical Islam?"

In answer to that question he offers an arresting anecdote of village youths resolving a dispute not through the modern legal bureaucracy but by using masqueraders and masks "as agents of law enforcement and coercion." The anecdote points to an important difference between African and European cultures. Monotheism is less deeply rooted in the former; the old beliefs, although facing erosion, persist in subtle and unanticipated ways. The evidence of this can be found in the ambiguity of personages and characters in many African and Caribbean masquerades.

Olufemi Terry won the 2010 Caine Prize for African writing for his short story "Stickfighting Days." His essays and fiction have been published in the *American Scholar*, *Guernica,* and *Chimurenga*. He has been writer in residence at Georgetown and Cove Park.

There are hardly any statues that do not seek to turn back time, tweets Achille Mbembe. Colonial effigies testify to this mute genealogy.

Stacy Hardy, critic

# An Essential Gesture of Cultural Resistance

*A roundtable conversation between Misheck Masamvu from Village Unhu in Zimbabwe, members of lugar a dudas, and Adriana Quiñones León from Afrorexistencia, both in Colombia, moderated by Aïcha Diallo*
*Saturday, October 22, 2016*

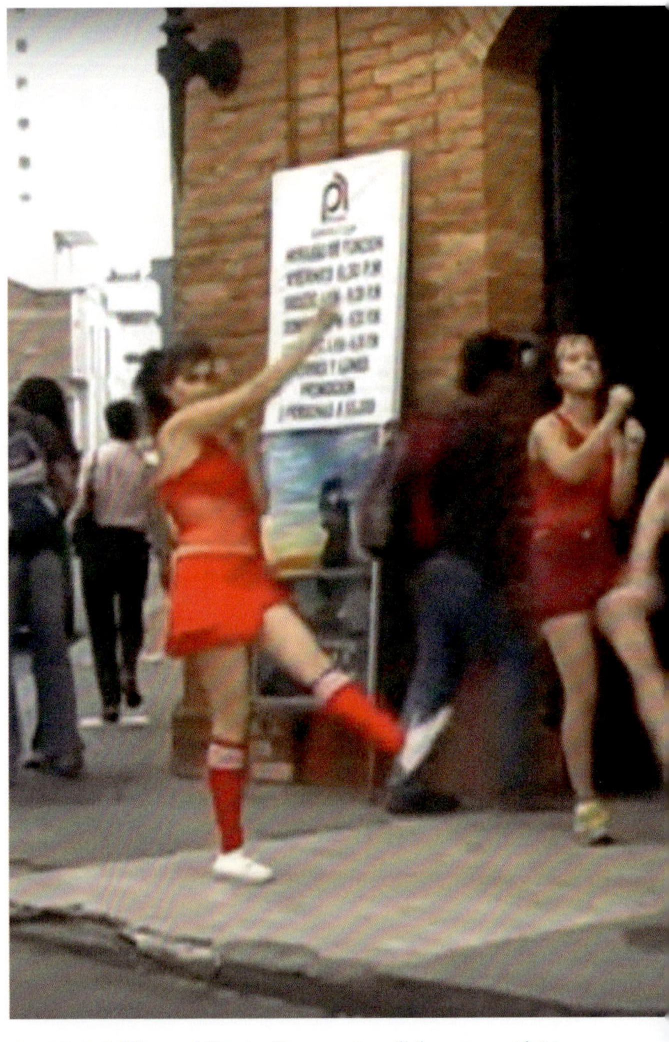

Ana Maria Millan and Monica Restrepo in collaboration with Liga Femenina de Baile, *Cali Choreography Dancing Show*, 2008. Public performance. Screenshot taken from calichoreography by Proartes (YouTube)

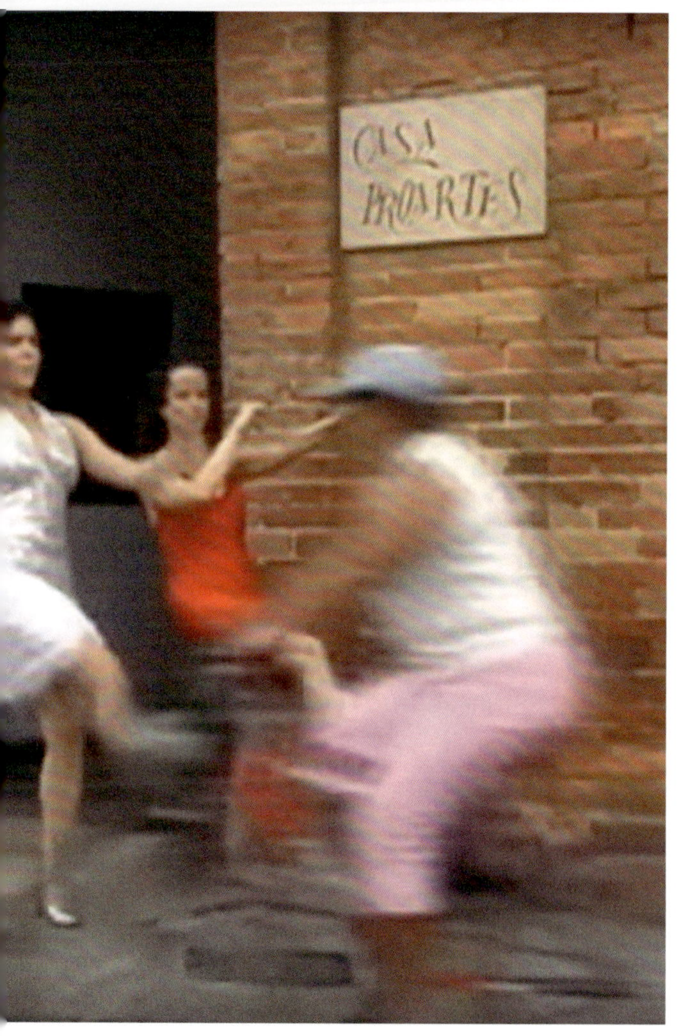

CASA
PROARTES

*Aïcha Diallo:* Being artists, why did you choose to (co-)create an art space?

*Misheck Masamvu:* We once created Artist in Conversation, an intervention to speak about the ills imposed by institutions against the artist. It was a good platform that however ended in a disaster and unnecessary jabbering. I learned from it that real talk is when you present a product and talk about the product rather than speak for or against an idea that is still in the imagination. We strongly believe that some form of a structure has to be built by artists around their practice, enabling them to develop organically, not to have their work informed or prescribed by institutions or market forces.

*Adriana Quiñones León:* The collective Afro-rexistencia emerges from the desire and vital need of its members to set forth on a path of collective action that utilizes artistic languages and practices and social communication to contribute to the transformation of the unjust realities experienced by Global South communities. To this end, Afrorexistencia inscribes itself as a chapter of this creative duty and impulse where the protagonist and historical subject is of African descent.

*lugar a dudas:* lugar a dudas opened as an attempt to respond to the needs of the city of Cali's art scene in a historical moment when, despite the frenetic activity of several groups of artists, there weren't

spaces to show their work nor initiatives that supported their practices. Institutions at the time, more
than now, ignored those artists and acted based
on populism, without a clue of what cultural policies
were about. So the project started as a gesture
of cultural resistance. While the idea of creating
a space was initiated by Oscar Muñoz and Sally
Mizrachi, its implementation is the result of a
collective effort. The project has been built over
a decade with the participation of many artists and
people who have contributed from different perspectives and disciplines to create possibilities for
exchange and dialogue. We encourage readers to
check out the list of our residents and guest artists
on our website, lugaradudas.org.

Also, lugar a dudas has benefited from the
support and collaboration of relevant artists from
Cali who have been part of the staff, coordinating
all of our activities and making effective decisions
defined through dialogue and group negotiation.
Our goal is to foster an inclusive community rather
than only a platform for the promotion of a few,
so that's our reason to avoid, among other things,
dropping certain names rather than others.

Over the years we've been exploring different
courses of action; we've joined networks and experi-
mented around cross-practice, participatory
platforms and formats to expand the ways in which

the artists can show their work and interact with their audiences.

*Aïcha Diallo:* Could you share the vision and the goals of your art platforms?

*Misheck Masamvu:* The vision is quite a difficult one to realize. The goals on the other hand are very simple. The goal is to improve our reality and conditions. Currently, Village Unhu offers studio spaces and accommodation as a residency program hosting artists for a maximum of three months. We have a created a contemporary exhibition and gallery space. The vision is to have a group of people or, at this stage, artists who ask questions and under-stand that not every question needs to be answered in words. Through our work, we stand a chance to initiate a new turn of events or experiences. The vision goes beyond encouraging the artists to keep their doors open to others in need. Through the platform we have a chance to look within ourselves and learn about others.

*Adriana Quiñones León:* Afrorexistencia endeavors to recover Afro-Colombian historical memory through paleography and ethnography while facilitating the re-appropriation of these memories—through diverse artistic, audio-musical, visual, and written languages—by the very communities they belong to.

*lugar a dudas:* Beyond the visibility of tangible artistic products, which, of course, is an essential part of our interest, lugar a dudas places particular emphasis on issues that arise in today's society with the intention of highlighting different points of view, bringing out contradictions and divergences to generate complexity and critical thought.

The space, an art center that includes a documentation center, exhibition rooms, a residency program, film screenings, seminars, workshops, and more, is currently redefining its vision towards the integration of the art scenes in the city with a broader community of academics, thinkers, social practitioners, writers, youth scenes, and other communities that act as cultural agents. Starting from the consensus of what an artist is supposed to do, we are trying to create spaces where these assumptions are challenged, transformed, and redefined. In order to do this, we are enhancing our organization as a space for education, discussion, and criticality. Under the motto "Educación sin Escuela" (Education without School), we're trying to explore new avenues, looking for fresh experiences, partners, and chances to learn from our mistakes and actions.

*Aïcha Diallo:* Please tell us a little bit about the names of your platforms: Village Unhu, Afrorexistencia, and lugar a dudas.

*Misheck Masamvu:* The original name for Village Unhu was supposed to be "dunhu unhu." We then

settled for Village Unhu. Village at this stage does
not refer to a "locus," it is a "munyati," an idea of
collecting and unpacking various views and experiences. Just as the saying "a child is born to be raised
by everyone," although our stories might speak
on the individual experience, the story is often about
everyone. Unhu is not an idea or concept; Unhu is
a footprint of humanity.

*Adriana Quiñones León:* The name Afrorexistencia
makes reference to the varied and new forms of existence established by descendants of the African
Diaspora in the particular regions they settled, as
well as the ways they resisted enslavement, erasure,
discrimination, and exploitation.

*lugar a dudas:* lugar a dudas means "room for
doubt," a name that, undoubtedly, claims the right
to think twice, to never be comfy in any position,
to exercise a healthy opposition while hesitating, even
about doubt and negativity, by the exercise of action,
organization, and cultural production. To have
some room for doubt doesn't imply stopping and
refusing. Is not a state of inaction but a statement
in defense of the provisional.

*Aïcha Diallo:* How would you describe the artistic
community in your respective context? How do
you engage with it?

*Misheck Masamvu:* I know there are lots of creative, sensitive people in Harare; I am not sure if they

would find me suitable to speak on their behalf.
The artist community in Harare is sensitive and
above all it is sensible to rise above one's precarious
realities.

*Adriana Quiñones León:* We can think about the
Afro-Colombian artistic community as a social
actor that expresses itself through idioms, forms of
knowledge, and traditional expressions that some
call folkloric, and that are transformed by history
and take on new forms. We understand our contribution as a revisionist historical perspective on
Afro-Colombian cultural history. For example, we
are currently preparing an illustrated publication
that is the product of rigorous ethnographic archival
research, but that utilizes a visual and written
language accessible to any audience. This publication
seeks to articulate the memory and identities
of people of African descent suppressed by colonial
processes, because we believe that "the shortest path
to the future is a profound knowledge of the past."

*lugar a dudas:* Cali is a city with a population
of 2.5 million. The city has an art museum, two
commercial galleries, and five professional arts programs, each of them with different approaches.
The lack of structured cultural policies has resulted
in a wide range of needs in the different artist communities all over the city. Artists respond to this institutional precariousness through self-organization,

DIY ethics, temporary initiatives, and, in general, a rich set of informal practices. lugar a dudas works locally, fostering artists' initiatives and facilitating access to information, knowledge, and possibilities to reinforce these different local initiatives, as well as their ways to interact in meaningful ways.

*Aïcha Diallo:* With reference to your many forms of collaboration, can you talk a bit about how you see the role of education in your artistic practice and in relation to your art space?

*Misheck Masamvu:* The role of education could be seen as a sham. The role of educating has been reduced to transferring information without it translating from real experiences. To dwell only on words and speak of a quotable history is to neglect one's present reality and experience. We must work, even if your work is to speak from the heart about what you know, not as you have been told.

*Adriana Quiñones León:* The place of cultural education and arbitration is fundamental, thus it is necessary to draw connections between academic intellectual production and other epistemic subjects through the mediation of artistic languages in the codification/decodification of discourse.

*lugar a dudas:* It has been crucial for us to strengthen the relationship between artistic and pedagogical practices. We incorporated the slogan "Educación sin Escuela" as a statement that guides our action and unifies our mission, offering space and opportunities for practitioners to implement new forms of work and organization; to build networks; to connect the local to an international community of cultural agents, institutions, and peers; and, finally, to produce complex layers of thought, practice, and affection.

We are learning to learn from those who come to learn from the space. We are thinking about entanglement, about the need to effect and being affected by others at a distance.

*Aïcha Diallo:* Misheck, can you tell us a little bit about your contribution to the 32nd Bienal de São Paulo?

*Misheck Masamvu:* The work can only be painted at night, usually around midnight. It has become a ritual. It seems like time stands still, a time undecided. My work is about doubt about to reach a clear state of mind. To commit to a life's worth, defying the risen night spirits.

*Aïcha Diallo:* How did you come up with this idea?

*Misheck Masamvu:* I guess I am frustrated to learn that knowledge drawn from fear imagined holds my reality hostage. Why must I live in fear of tomorrow?

Village Unhu is a creative art space taking part in the cultural and artistic production and development of the local art scene of Harare, Zimbabwe.

lugar a dudas is an independent non-profit space and laboratory aiming to support the creative processes of contemporary artists within the community. It is based in Cali, Colombia.

Afrorexistencia is an art collective which utilizes the artistic languages, perspectives, and practices of its members to transform the lived realities of communities of the Global South. Afrorexistencia set out to bring (historical) collective memories out of their obscurity and anonymity by creating an information platform to enhance the dialogue of diverse memories. They are based in Colombia.

# The Flexible Methodologies of Unathi Sigenu

*By Gugulective*
*Friday, January 31, 2014*

Born in 1977 in Cape Town, Unathi Sigenu was an award-winning multimedia artist with political awareness. His artistic practice focused on installations, paintings, performances, and videos primarily exploring themes revolving around urban context and violence. Sigenu was also a founding member of the renowned artist collective Gugulective, based in the Gugulethu township. Gugulective was initiated as a platform situated in the intersection between art and political activism. Sigenu participated in numerous residencies and exhibitions in South Africa and at an international level. Unathi Sigenu passed away in Cape Town in late December 2013.

—

"Do you know who these guys are?" asked the policeman. It was almost midnight after a long day of preparation for a Gugulective show. We were walking Kemang home when the police stopped us and searched us. They found marijuana in Unathi's pocket. Peculiarly, they tried forcing him to eat it. He refused. Then we were all manhandled and violently thrown into the back of a police van. After all, we were guilty, not only of carrying marijuana but for being Black. We attempted to negotiate, but our words fell on deaf ears.

"Do you know who these guys are?" insisted another cop, turning to his colleagues. "I know these guys," the policeman gave the answer himself

And so Empire
The Rijks continues
Declaring
It wasn't US
Not us
Not we
Not now
Continuing to make
  itself, They.

Thato Magano, writer

at the lack of a reply from his colleagues. "I have been
following their art activities here in the neighborhood.
These guys are part of the Black Consciousness
Movement. Do you know the Black Consciousness
Movement? They are more powerful than the ANC
(African National Congress) but there are not more
than twenty of them in their group." After those
words, we were released and didn't encounter any
further incidents. The policeman was referring
to Gugulective.

First, Unathi Sigenu was our friend, brother,
comrade, and everything to us. He was a painter
and multimedia artist. Ma-Uni, as he was known
by those closest to him, grew up in the 1980s
in the tumultuous and tear-gas-ridden streets of
Gugulethu, a township located on the Cape Flats.
Cape Flats designates the low-lying, flat area
situated on the outskirts of Cape Town as a reserve
for cheap labor of Black and colored people.
Unathi witnessed the terror and violence meted out
against his people in those days. He also saw the
beast of apartheid being dismantled in those
slippery streets. And the subsequent betrayal and
exclusion of those very Black multitudes in
so-called post-apartheid South Africa. He was dis-
gusted by it!

When Sigenu was eighteen, he was involved in
a fight that claimed the life of one of the participants.

He was arrested and spent the next ten years mainly in Malmesbury Correctional Prison where he also matriculated. While in prison, he joined the Buddhist faith and practiced Zen meditation together with fourteen other inmates as a means of self-rehabilitation. He also started making art, developed a love of reading, and dreamed of being an artist. He and Kemang Wa Lehulere co-founded the Cape Town-based arts collective Gugulective in 2006. The collective was driven by the need to form an alternative creative space that would animate intellectual and creative dialogues as well as other enriching possibilities outside of the often bourgeois mainstream art world. With Unathi as our unofficial leader, we opened geographic as well as cognitive spaces that were deserted in the peripheries of contemporary South Africa. To date, Gugulective has curated its own projects from its "adopted" space, a local *shebeen* (bar) called Kwa-Malmli's in Gugulethu, and also participated in numerous exhibitions and festivals locally and internationally.

In his personal capacity, Unathi participated in numerous projects locally and internationally, including seminars, conferences, and workshops. His interactive *Police Jacket* (2012) remains one of his most exciting projects. In the middle of downtown Johannesburg, Sigenu installed a police jacket (which had belonged to his late brother, who was in the police service and died in the line of duty) with a sound installation hidden inside it.

What was in the jacket was a two-way police radio or a walkie-talkie, as we commonly call it. He loved his work and was always interested in ideas that encouraged multiple ways of seeing. Though his concepts focused on typical subjects, they were all tied to his fixation on multidimensionality and the polyvalence of objects. Looking at things from the same angle all the time was something that greatly troubled him. His first solo show at the Association for Visual Arts Gallery (AVA) titled "Diminished Man" (2012) "explored the representation of the human body.  Body functions, body language, gestures and the politics of the body." More recently he collaborated with fellow Gugulective member, Khanyisile Mbongwa, in their installation, *Die Kat*, which was part of the MTN New Contemporaries Award.

Sigenu was a typical example of a "contemporary" artist in the fullest sense of the word—he was not adverse to improvisation; he valorized it. Yet his being in the moment did not mean he was unbalanced or free-floating. In 2008 he staged a spontaneous "unauthorized march" in the streets of Johannesburg with the radical Black consciousness group Blackwash. He treated rigidity and flexibility with the sophistication of dialectics.

He was most at peace with jazz and the blues, and his love for Cassandra Wilson was unparalleled. His love for music was not ritualistic. That is, he would not put on music to disrupt silence; his ear was always searching. He was also a gentleman in the old-fashioned sense—his love for clothing (for quality, not excess) wasn't an empty veneration of vulgar materialism. He was meticulous—a shirt wasn't something he wrapped his body in, it had to be the real thing. This meticulousness translated into his life, his living and working spaces. His love for detail was impeccable yet had a Zen-like quality that made it all seem easy. Unathi Sigenu had his weaknesses like any of us. He was overprotective and was never swayed by the fact that he was the oldest in the Gugulective. It would come up on occasion, suffused in echoes of laughter. Unathi leaves behind his mother and two sisters, to whom he was very close. He leaves his friends, colleagues and lots of people who looked up to him.

Unathi was found dead in his apartment in Cape Town on December 25, 2013.

We will always miss you, dear brother, wherever you are. Your brotherly love for us will always sing in our hearts. Your ability to not shy away from the power of imagination will always be the biggest highlight in all of our lives. Gugulective will continue to thrive, dream your dreams, and create in these difficult times. Rest in peace, Ma-Uni.

Gugulective is an art collective based in Cape Town. Founded in the township of Gugulethu (today a suburb of Cape Town) in 2006, the collective brings together actors, dancers, performers, musicians, DJs, rappers, and poets and works with various media, such as painting, photography, film, video, and animation.

# Love as a Public Act in São Paulo

*By Lucélia Sergio and Sidney Santiago Kuanza*
*Saturday, October 22, 2016*

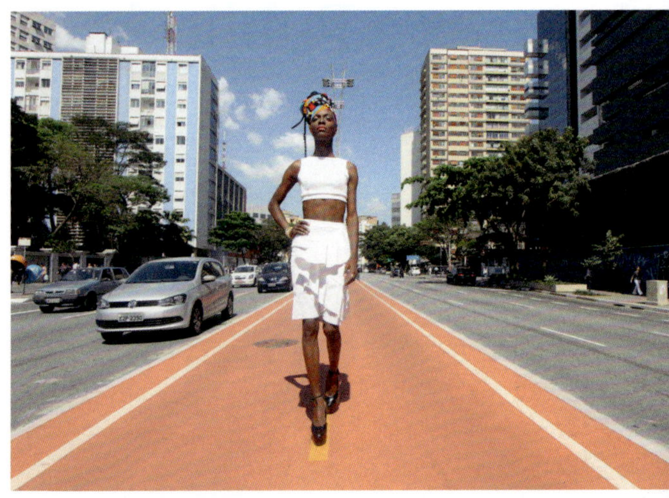

Aretha Sadick performing on Paulista Avenue, the main street of São Paulo, 2015. Courtesy of Nabor Jr. Photo: Mandela Crew

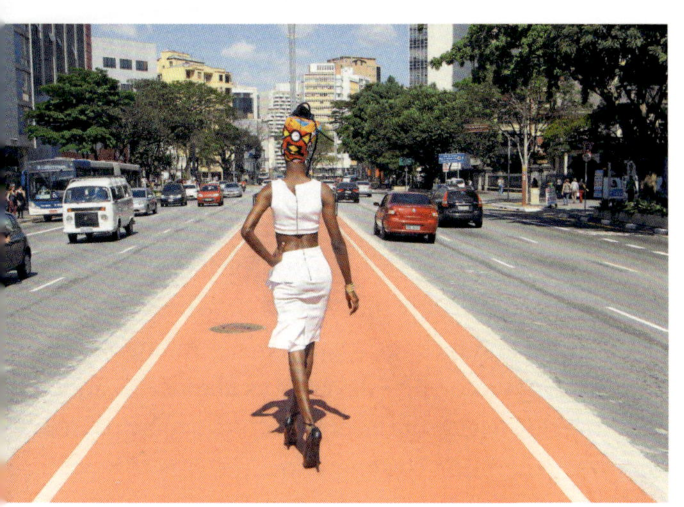

Viewing love as a priority in Black lives is a rather complex maneuver because it compels us to question our very emotions. We will likely encounter serious emotional barriers in terms of what we mean by strength, sharing, or hiding feelings, the need for affection—often at odds with the exigencies of day-to-day survival—and, finally, the choices and desires that ultimately make us who we are.

Racism and feelings of supremacy among whites did not evaporate once slavery was abolished, and the lingering legacy of slavery continues to be passed on from generation to generation in terms of how we love. According to bell hooks, the Black feminist writer from the United States, "we think we'll jeopardize our survival if we let ourselves go and yield to our emotions." That is what we learned from a slave system: to dismantle our affective ties. We were forced to believe that we only have control over our lives when we repress our emotions or pay little or no attention to our families, not giving them any affection, or when we teach our kids and siblings not to cry when they witness racism or discrimination. When affection is considered to be as important as survival and the fight against racism, we come to realize that oppression and forms of domination have compromised the very existence of Black people. When racism impacts emotional health and feelings, it leaves permanent marks and weakens us to the point that we are unable to fight for who we are.

As a symbolic field of imagined sociabilities, art opens a space for possibilities and experimentation with other tangible realities. Accordingly, many artists have explored issues related to emotional life and its interplay with society, especially emotions and identities that depart from the norm. In this context, we as researchers at Cia: Os Crespos de Teatro e Intervenção completed an audiovisual survey of stagecraft (2011–2015) that delves into the emotional lives of Black women and men, examining how slavery impacts on our ways of loving. Entitled *Dos Desmanches aos Sonhos: Poética em Legítima Defesa* (From Wrecks to Dreams: Poetry as Self-Defense), the project, conceived under the City of São Paulo's theater funding program Programa Municipal de Fomento ao Teatro, involved research, production, and a five-show tour. In an attempt to create poetry that transcends this boundary, we have focused on our experience as an "encounter" in order to understand emotional contexts and diverse identities. Field research spanned bars, porn movie theaters, squares, diversity centers, offices, prisons, households, and a myriad of other physical spaces in São Paulo, where researchers engaged with women, men, transvestites, cross-dressers, drag queens, and transgender people of varying ages, though

The function of the imagination is not to make strange things settled, so much as to make settled things strange.

G. K. Chesterton, poet, philosopher

contact was predominantly with younger individuals.
Based on the listening experience, Os Crespos created
a show that assembled the interviews alongside the
mythical and transgressive figure of Madame Satã
(Madam Satan, 1900–1976), a Pernambucan trans-
vestite who spent part of her life in Rio de Janeiro.
Cartas à Madame Satã Ou Me Desespero Sem
Notícias Suas (Letters to Madame Satã, or, Hopeless
Growing Desperate without Hearing from You) sets
out to create a discourse in favor of love, while also
discussing themes such as emotional life. The work
also crafts a poetic statement in which love as a
public act is considered to be a fight for one's identity.

—

*Head-On*

From the beginning, Cia Os Crespos has treated performance as a space for the body's intervention
and the audience's relationship with the body. In
this sense, the performance of certain artists has
laid bare their experience as witness to an emotional
life hemmed in by taboos. This body/witness not
only represents the realm of potential affect, but also
serves as a statement, a claim, and a debate. With
more than 14,000 Facebook likes, the Tumblr called
Bicha Nagô, created to expose previously hush-hush
situations, shares everyday experiences as a safe
space for discussing themes of sexuality and race.
Using social networking, performer Ézio Rosa

has branched out into artistic events organized to discuss the subject.

Rico Dalasam, hailing from Taboão da Serra in the state of São Paulo, has gained acclaim in various countries and recently released a new album, *Orunga* (2016). Emerging from legendary rap competitions regularly held at the Santa Cruz metro station in São Paulo, the rapper continues to weave groundbreaking narratives within hip-hop culture. Embracing the principle that such culture was popularized for expressing unfiltered truth, Dalasam decided to talk about being gay, how he loves, how he sees himself within society, and, in turn, how society views him.

In his experiment against homophobia entitled *Meninos Também Amam—Um poema/manifesto cênico* (Boys Love Too: An On-Stage Poem/Manifesto), Inacaba Cia.'s Rafael Guerche has boldly attempted to build drama and staging that can open up a space for affection among equals. In the creative milieu of young theater students, his initiative is poetically striking, showing nude figures making love in public, unleashing love and emotion.

The actor, performer, and costume designer Robson Rozza—as he calls himself—was once an introverted, introspective child. Nevertheless, the lanky boy has transformed himself into a restless, fearless presence who won over the world.

Robson is the artist behind the persona Aretha Sadick Drag Queen, who is recognized not only for elaborate artistic performances but also for not shying away from speaking out about social insertion and civil rights. In a drama class at the Martins Pena School, the artist and his classmates formed a research and language collective in which he assumed the acting role. His interpretation of a monologue inspired by the feminine universe explored in the songs of Brazil's famed singer-songwriter Chico Buarque drew the attention of a friend who urged him to wear the outfit created by the renowned Paranaense designer Henrique Filho for the 22nd edition of Miss Gay Rio de Janeiro, which he won. "It was totally unexpected and unplanned … The contest won me a 'pass,' and I could have seized on more opportunities from that. But I wanted to distance myself from that world. I was very young," he has said. He retreated to his studies in fashion (which gave way to theater) and began working in art education. He was an artist in residence at the 2012 London Summer Olympics, where he had the opportunity to explore gay London nightlife and experience other contexts and aspects in the world of cross-dressing, transvestites, and drag queens. Just after he returned to Brazil, a friend who was organizing Rebola—a touring music festival—invited the artist to perform. "Aretha was dormant and no

longer relevant then, but she made a comeback at that festival and came back onto the scene."
Against all odds and—literally—not dropping the ball, Robson and Aretha remain one, sharing the same body and ideas. The artist currently participates in Drag-se, a collective of young Rio artists with a YouTube channel that takes a weekly, behind-the-scenes glimpse into the world of drag artists, raising awareness and urging the need for visibility and dialogue related to multiple identities. "I'm trying to merge my knowledge of the performing arts, costumes, fashion design, and discussions on sexuality and gender. Like I said, I'm now Aretha Sadick the Drag Queen, but first and foremost I'm Robson Rozza, an artist."

Lucélia Sergio is an actress and founding member of Cia Os Crespos, a theater collective of scenic and audiovisual research, debates, and public interventions, composed of Black actors.

Sidney Santiago Kuanza is an actor and founding member of the group Cia Os Crespos.

Text commissioned by *O Menelick 2° Ato*

# Ensuring That We See Ourselves

*A conversation between EJ Hill and Magnus Rosengarten*
*Tuesday, February 21, 2017*

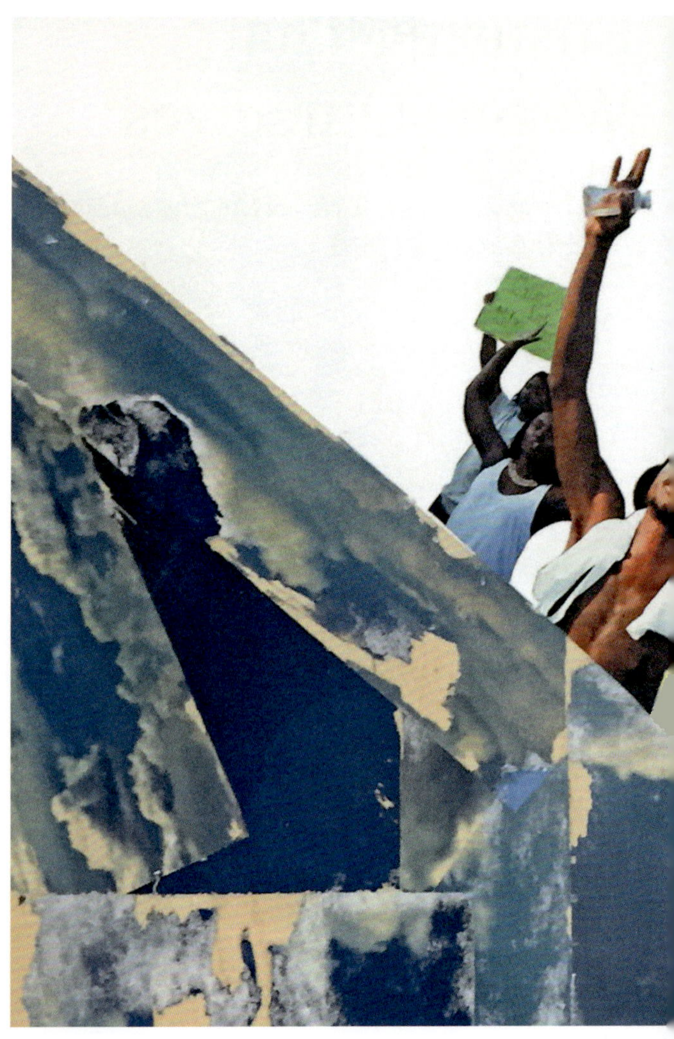

EJ Hill, *Surrendered (A Harrowing Descent)*, 2016. Acrylic, collage, and photo transfer on birch panel. Courtesy of the Studio Museum in Harlem

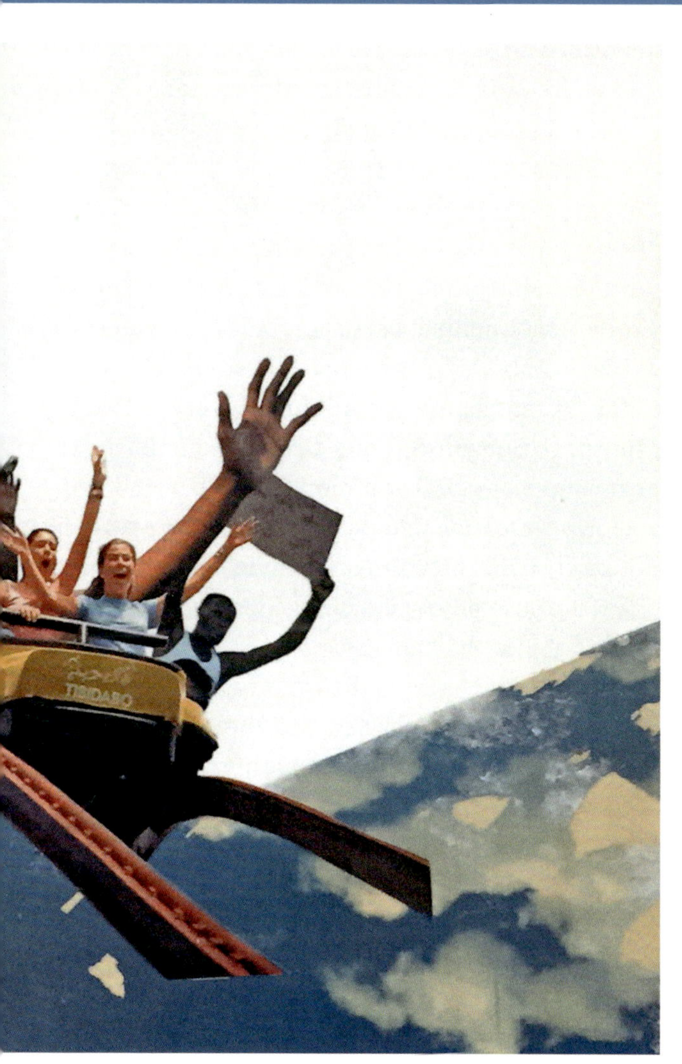

Renowned artists who have lived in the US for decades told us they are seriously considering not returning to the US as long as Donald Trump is in power. An influential curator from New York emailed us the day of the election, still completely in shock: "Winter in America. It's certainly tough here. But folks feel ready to fight!" We have received many similar statements by artists, curators, academics, writers—emotional, powerful, concerned reactions to the current status quo. In the new series "Don't Mourn, Organize!" our question to them during the next couple of weeks and months will be: How can we form a creative perspective, how do we react by not solely concentrating on the uncertainties and crises but instead transforming ideas into platforms and strategies for change?

*C&:* James Hetfield, the front man of Metallica, recently said in an interview that the vote for Trump would not change anything about his work because he did not want to give this new government the power to influence his artistic work. What is your perspective on this in terms of your art? Will the vote impact your work?

*EJ Hill:* This vote will most definitely impact my work, but I am not sure to what degree. David Hammons once said that he doesn't really like art at all, that he is more concerned with symbols, and art is just one context for engaging with, or challenging, the power of symbols. This election isn't about one man or his administration. This is about everything he and his supporters symbolize, what they represent. And let's be honest, what they represent is as old as America itself. So will the results of this election impact my work? Yes, undoubtedly, but I imagine the impact to be similar to that of November 7, 2016. Or like, any other Monday prior.

*C&:* What is your perspective on America's current condition, your perspective as a citizen, as an artist? After all, is it really that new and unprecedented?

*EJ Hill:* Exactly, no, none of this is new at all! And I think that's what's been the most frustrating part about all of this for me. The fact is that a lot of us—Black people specifically—have been living within this reality for a very long time, and fighting against it for just as long, but now that so-called left-leaning white people feel threatened, there seems to be a particular kind of urgency, a certain trend toward action. And it's difficult sometimes not to view this all as some bizarre tagging-out-of-the-ring, you know? Part of me is thinking, "Where the hell have you been?" but the other part of me is saying, "Okay, your turn."

*C&:* As a performance artist, what role does your body play in your practice? What is your relationship to it?

*EJ Hill:* For me, performance is grounded in the attempt to negotiate the constant push and pull between presence and absence. And when you exist in a body that is rendered invisible by racist, heterosexist, misogynist, classist, or ableist structures, hyper-visibility becomes the paradoxical rule. It's almost like, "You see me everywhere because you're trying so hard not to," and so, much of my performance work is in direct response to this. It's important for me to insert my body into physical or ideological spaces where I may not be warmly welcomed, to ensure that I am seen, but perhaps more importantly, to ensure that we see ourselves.

*C&:* Do you see any healing or curative potential in performance art or practices that involve the body as an immediate instrument? Is there potential for more immediate contact with audiences?

*EJ Hill:* Yes, performance is almost medicinal in that way. Any time we're dealing with our bodies, we're dealing with every scratch, bump, and pulse that it has ever experienced—we carry all of our physical and psychological echoes in our skins, our bones, everywhere we go. And if we don't release some of that every once in a while, or transform it in some way, we might actually be a little worse off.

As far as contact with audiences goes, I don't think my presence or action in the museum or gallery or art contexts in general is that effective or

immediate, as these spaces are generally operating
within the same prohibitive power structures
as many other institutions in contemporary society.
Action around the dinner table with family, action
at the grocery store, gas station, on the sidewalk,
or on the subway—where the people are—that's where
the gold is. That's where the potential for presence
to resonate exponentially is the highest.

*C&:* What is sexuality to you? How does it inform
your art?

*EJ Hill:* I could literally spend the rest of my life
elaborating on this question! But following up on
your previous question, sexuality might actually be
the most healing and restorative space. People forget that sexuality doesn't necessarily have to include
sexual acts. It's also the space of desire, attraction,
fantasies, repressions, and traumas. And all that
manifests in different ways. So when we share ourselves intimately, it's like a tacit request to be cared
for and to hold or regard all that we bring with us
as valuable. We're entrusting others to help undo
what has been done to our bodies. But sometimes
they further reinforce what we're trying to get away
from, and that risk is all part of the healing process.
It takes huge amounts of courage to continually
readjust the dials on our desires and to tweak our
dosages in an attempt to find that perfect remedy,
that bliss.

*C&:* As Toni Morrison reminded us recently, this is the time to get back to work as an artist. What will you be working on specifically in the coming months, and years, perhaps?

*EJ Hill:* I like to meditate on a certain mantra or theme when I'm producing a body of work. Last year, while in residence at the Studio Museum, I had a piece of blue painter's tape on an inconspicuous part of my desk and on it I had written the words: "A monumental offering of potential energy." It eventually became the title for the work I showed in our exhibition "Tenses." Now, I have a sheet of paper taped to my studio wall that reads: "The necessary reconditioning of the highly deserving." I'm not sure if it is a titular move just yet, but I'm definitely approaching new works (sculptures and paintings mostly) that nod to elevation and the imperativeness in so many of us to be able to see ourselves way, way up.

Magnus Rosengarten is a filmmaker, journalist, and writer from Germany. He lives in New York City and is currently pursuing his M.A. in Performance Studies at NYU.

# Whose Oyster is This World?

*By Orlando Reade*
*Sunday, February 10, 2013*

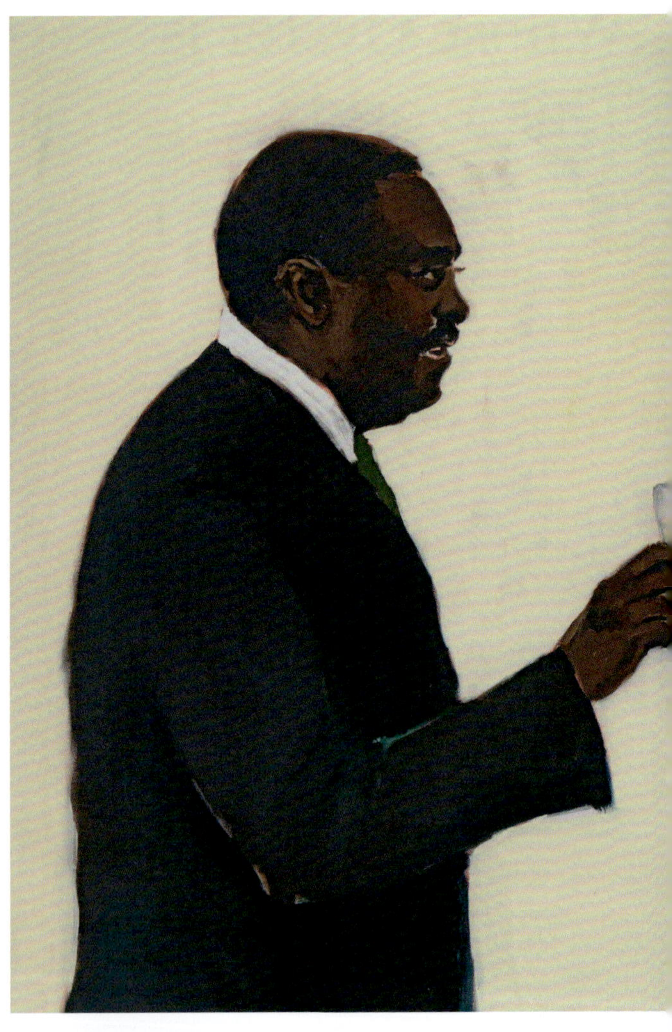

Lynette Yiadom-Boakye, *Songs in the Head* (detail), 2012. Oil on canvas. Courtesy of Corvi-Mora, London, and Jack Shainman Gallery, New York

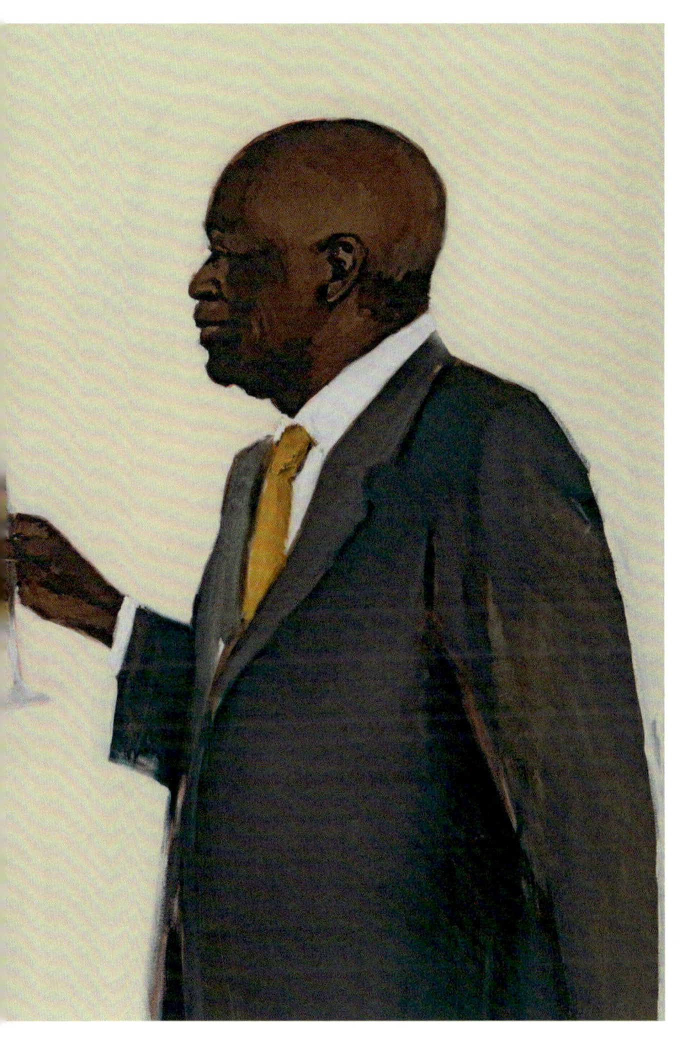

*Lynette Yiadom-Boakye's work has brought success and attention in recent years from contemporary art's most influential critics and institutions, but her paintings guard a kind of uncertainty which troubles close attention.*

I am travelling on a night bus through the university town in which I am a resident, and as we wind through the midwinter mist which descended just after midnight, a conversation begins with the only other passenger.

We look at some books of Sufi poetry I have borrowed from the library and he starts to tell me about his childhood in Iran, his Islamic upbringing, and how he lost his faith when he started to study theoretical physics. He doesn't consider himself a practicing Muslim, but often still prays, to a God, and has started meditation. After one intense meditation, an Indian technique whose name I don't catch, he experienced what is called astral projection —his face looms up, across the bus aisle, close to mine, his eyebrows are sincerely raised—his mind became free from his body; did not altogether depart from it, but remained, like a balloon rubbing up against the ceiling, "not far, but far." He is no longer certain that physics, the science of bodies, has an answer for everything.

There is a history of uncertainty—theorized for mathematics by Werner Heisenberg, scattered as words across a white page by Stéphane Mallarmé and the poets of free verse, drawn out in the indeterminacies of modernist abstraction, and reclaimed for portraiture by Francis Bacon—the power and significance of which are newly realised in the work of Lynette Yiadom-Boakye, in whose paintings uncertainty is manifest as a dialectic of light and darkness. The artist, born to British-Ghanaian parents in 1977, has produced a body of work more interesting —to this viewer at least—than any other painter of her generation. She has won various lucrative prizes, she has high-profile exhibitions in New York, London, and Cape Town, and her paintings now sell for many thousands of pounds. This success is unquestionable according to the logic of contemporary art, but her paintings guard an uncertainty which troubles our attention, prohibits easy conclusions about what they mean, and may prove to be critical to the work's unsettling power.

Consider the painting *Oyster*: The subject of this painting is a body presented to the viewer as an arrangement of dark areas wrapped in the brushstrokes of a whitish dressing-gown. The body is delineated thickly against the dirty off-whites of the back wall and floor, an almost crude pastiche of the smooth backgrounds of Velázquez or Manet. The body, perched on the edge of a lush red armchair in elegant flat shoes, looks like a celebrity in a dressing-room, accepting of portrayal, one hand placed patiently atop the other. The face, however, has an enthusiasm which betrays the body. The thick black shadows which the body's torso throws onto the wall behind suggest the effect of a photographic flash. Photography's emphasis on the bodily features of the subject and disinterest in the rest of the world are, however, absent here; the brushwork used to represent this body does not offer the narcissistic attentions that photography promises. The indeterminacy of these paintings offers a satirical mirror to the racism of cameras.

The interplay of light and darkness in this painting induces in the viewer an uncertainty which is central to the power of these paintings. Where the viewer of an equally large oil painting in a national art gallery would expect to recognize the signifiers which guide looking—the sociological facts of gender, sexuality, class, name, affect—Yiadom-Boakye's portraits offer only uncertainty. Who—or what—is "Oyster"? A parochial viewer might think of the Oyster cards of the smooth and expensive London transport system; we might hear Zora Neale Hurston sharpening her "oyster knife"; I remain uncertain whose world this oyster is. If it is a name, "Oyster" doesn't confirm the subject's gender, but its aphrodisiac connotations, the sympathetic magic of its shape's correspondent, signal the erotics of uncertainty.

It is unclear whether this body is male or female. This indeterminacy is central to art's radical calling-into-question of identity politics.

The last poem in the *Bulaq Diwan* of Ibn al-'Arabi, "I Saw Males in Females," alternates between masculine and feminine constructions to produce a space where the revelation of truth is a new kind of bewilderment. The "indeterminate questions" posed by poetry or painting offer exemplary resistance to grammars—visual and linguistic—of the empire that fixes identities. The body represented in Oyster is drawn for the viewer and, simultaneously, the viewer is drawn in; this chiasmic figure is the world of uncertainty. To turn this lens on its head: what world is this body's oyster? Yiadom-Boakye's titles often have a poetics which doesn't entirely match the visual data of the painting, creating a non-meeting of meanings between title and painting, a semantic dissonance between name and image which describes a body whose identity is not determined. With echoes of Gertrude Stein in our mind, and Yiadom Boakye's work *Rose Neither Poetry* in our view, the artist responds: a painting is a painting is a painting is a painting.

The title of *Songs in the Head*, for example, invites and resists the attribution of meaning. In the painting, two men—one smiling slightly, the other plainly confident—face each other, touching their champagne flutes together. The men's heavy suits, the affect of this encounter (if we can make a confident judgment), their pose, suggest a spirit of congratulation. In the dubious lens of the British media, the image of suited men engaged in champagne celebrations evokes, for this viewer at least, narratives of gluttony. Are these men the corrupt politicans that media portraits insist are unique to Africa? In Tony Blair's autobiography, that expert manipulator of mass media remarks on the naivety of his colleagues' decision to have themselves pictured at work with a bottle of wine. After New Labour's crusade to make "everyone" in Great Britain middle class, wine is less a spirit of aspiration than a commodity cheaply consumed by that same "everyone," and this reading falters. The men in Yiadom-Boakye's painting may be brothers, friends, or lovers.

Is the reason these paintings are so beguiling and so troubling the cognitive uncertainty they produce? The indeterminate space they create seems to accommodate a range of readings, naive and cynical, so that our response to them exposes us. The darknesses of these paintings, their dissonant names, evoke some hidden social commentary, but viewers who don't look for what is beyond this satirical mirror will find they have become its first victim. During her exhibition at the Chisenhale Gallery, the artist

I see myself as Sikán, since I am the observer, the mediator and the taleteller: I invent the images based on my studies and my experiences, since I am not a believer, and as I see her, I see myself.

Belkis Ayón, artist

was interviewed by the students of a local primary school; she gave the following answer to the question, "Why do you only paint people?"

"I find people really fun because you can do anything with them: paint them in their socks, make them dance, or just have them relaxing at the seaside."

This answer challenges the desire to overdetermine the meaning of these paintings, whose attention—to the almost inscrutable affects of single bodies, to the almost illegible relations between multiple bodies—recommends a gaze which sees in art a reflection of our needs. These speculations are, necessarily, as inconclusive as what is felt in front of these artworks and stolen away from the gallery into the rest of the world. If these uncertainties are the true work of these paintings, our task must be learning to live with them.

Orlando Reade writes about contemporary art and literature, and his writings have been published in *Africa Is a Country*, the *Guardian,* and *frieze*. He is currently a PhD candidate in English literature at Princeton University.

# An Eleventh-Hour Reckoning for Sudan's Golden Age

*By Clare Davies*
*Wednesday, June 3, 2015*

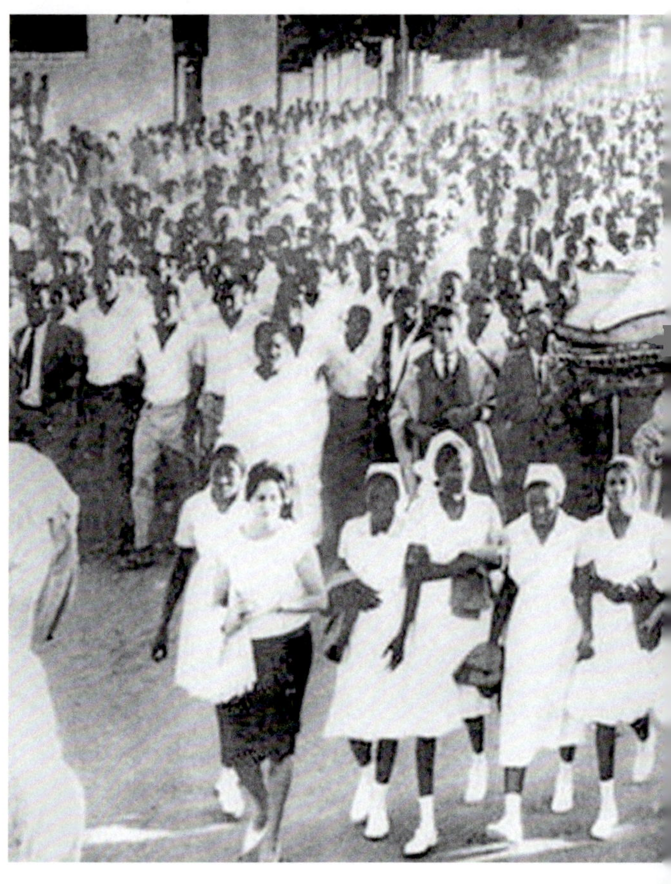

Scene from a procession during the October Revolution (Ahmad al-Qurashi's funeral, October 21, 1964). Courtesy of the Ministry of Culture, Republic of Sudan

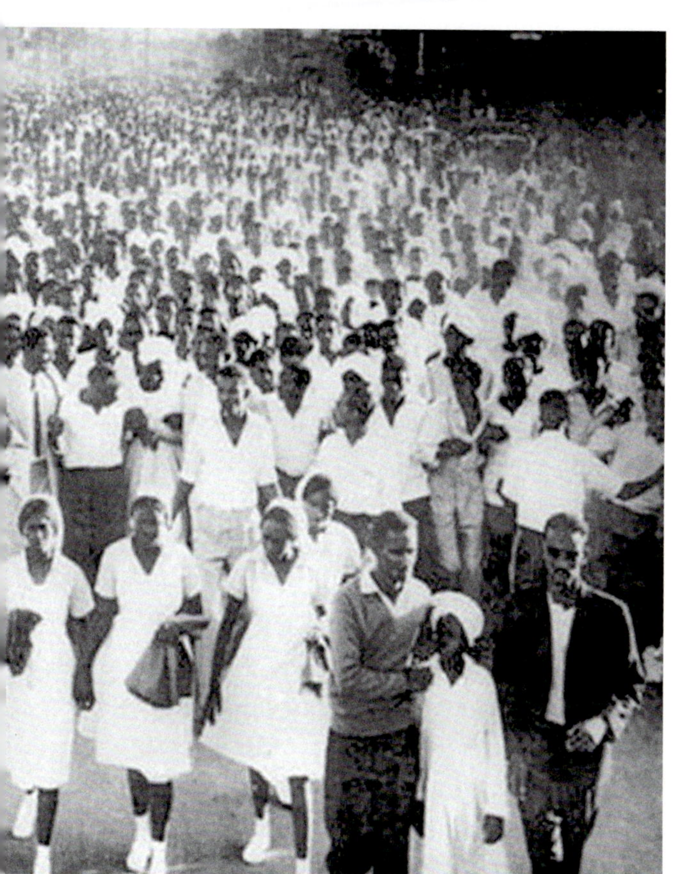

A generation of Sudanese civil society reconvened in Sharjah for a compressed, weekend-long reprise of a longstanding debate in April 2015.

"Modernity and the Making of Identity in Sudan: Remembering the Sixties and Seventies" offered an eleventh-hour reckoning for Sudan's cultural "golden age" and a generation of writers and artists who represent today both the period's exhilarating promise and the unrelenting disappointments marring subsequent decades. The scope and ambition of the proceedings made this a landmark event. For the first time, many of the period's main protagonists and their interlocutors convened in the same room to address questions that had critically shaped their respective careers and terms upon which the possibility (or impossibility) of a coherent modern Sudanese identity had historically been posited, namely a reconciliation of the country's "African" and "Arab" identities.

The advancing age of some of this generation's most influential figures threatens to cut short efforts at documentation and debate. The organizers succeeded in wringing every minute out of the two-and-a-half day symposium, packing in approximately forty papers and presentations related to the history of film, theater, cinema, music, and visual art of the period. I met people I'd only encountered in books or on museum walls; the contours of a decades-long conversation unfurled before my eyes in real time. The situation's poignancy was never more apparent than when Mohammed El Makki Ibrahim, author of the celebrated poem *Ummati* (My Nation, 1969), read some of his poems on stage while the audience recited his words along with him. Likewise, the charismatic solo presentations of artists Kamala Ibrahim Ishag and Amir Nour as well as theater director and playwright Shawgi Izzeldin Elamin elicited standing ovations and expressions of gratitude.

At other moments, however, this eulogy became an accusation: the symposium's success was a bitter reminder to some of the failures of those in attendance, who, they believed, could have made a difference sooner. "This is how they should have run the country," remarked the political cartoonist Khalid Albaih during a coffee break. Indeed, this sentiment echoed a conviction held by others I spoke to who believed that the Sudan's contemporary history of violence could be blamed, in part, on the failure of intellectuals to formulate a felicitous understanding of modern Sudanese identity. "It is now widely acknowledged that the issue of Sudan's cultural and political identity is one of the root causes of the Sudanese crises that has crippled the country since its independence in 1956 and plunged it into a civil war regarded as the longest in Africa," wrote

Mohamed Abusabib, another attendee, at the outset of his 2004 book *Art, Politics, and Cultural Identification in Sudan*. The secession of South Sudan in 2011 could not but represent the final collapse of former visions of a nation and national identity. In this regard, the stakes could hardly be higher.

The broad-strokes periodization that framed the symposium belied a more specific set of dates. Many participants pointed to the October Revolution of 1964 as a starting point that ushered in a brief window of relative stability and secular governance. Identifying an endpoint was more difficult and is perhaps better described not in relation to a particular moment, but rather as a confluence of events culminating in the consolidation of power within the hands of an authoritarian, Islamist government and the escalation of the Civil War in the 1980s. With one exception, an oddly depoliticized study of Hassan al-Turabi's "monotheistic" interpretation of identity and culture, this framework excluded any consideration of how Islamist rule in Sudan had informed cultural politics. Between 1964 and the 1980s, many of those present at the symposium had either held high-ranking posts in the government or been persecuted through imprisonment, forced exile, or other means (or had seen both favor and disfavor).

By and large, this symposium represented an extended conversation among a network of people

who had known each other for many years and were
intimately familiar with each other's work. Perhaps
as a result, there were few attempts to reconfigure or
make explicit some of the broader terms and
connections (for example the relationship between
the so-called Khartoum School of visual artists
and the literary School of the Jungle and the Desert
[Madrasat al-Ghaba wa-l-Sahra']) as promised by
the organizers. Some speakers rehearsed litanies of
significant historical events, while others presented
in-depth readings of a particular literary work,
reflected upon an important figure, or discussed a
major problematic attending the relationship of
"identity" to "modernity" in Sudan. The pace and
intensity of the proceedings required nothing short
of one's full attention. A battery of dense, fifteen-
minute presentations spanned a wide continuum of
topics and was spiced occasionally (I was told) with
coded references to longstanding quarrels.

Other axes of difference and disagreement were
more explicit. A generational divide distinguished
those who understood the postcolonial state as the
only viable framework within which to develop
cultural institutions (while also, at times, acknowl-
edging its dismal track record in doing so) from
those who actively sought alternatives. Tellingly, it
was only the founder of a major art space in Khartoum
whose easy relationship to the present status quo

seemed to absolve him of the discomforts of self-interrogation and intellectual critique. Instead, he used his time on stage to screen a promotional video for his space, geared, it seemed, towards potential fundraising, and ducked pointed questions from the audience regarding his hoarding of resources and exclusion of younger artists.

Two refrains recurred over the course of the three-day event in Sharjah: a call for self-criticism and the heralding of a new beginning for cultural discourse and practice in Sudan. Certainly, the organizers had knitted together various strands of a far-flung network spanning multiple generations and fields of practice with an eye to specific plans for the future. The event will serve as a platform for a series of exhibitions and publications co-produced by the Sharjah Art Foundation, directed by Sheikha Hoor al-Qasimi and the Institute for Comparative Modernities at Cornell University, headed by the art historian Salah Hassan. At least some of the participants seemed to feel the same way about the event's potential as a catalyst for future initiatives while wondering how it might be possible to bring the conversation "back" to Sudan. Meanwhile, it was the younger writers and artists in attendance who offered the most powerful arguments for self-reflectivity as an urgent ethical question and an intellectual position.

In the fifteen minutes allotted her, Stella Gaitano deftly shuffled off the cumbersome Arab-North/African-South binary with a probing reflection on her reception as a "South Sudanese" who writes in Arabic. Gaitano was born in Khartoum and graduated from the University of Khartoum in 2006, only moving to Juba, the capital of South Sudan, after 2011. Despite this personal history, she noted with a smile, people often expressed amazement at her ability to write in Arabic. Picking up where she left off, the final speaker, novelist and literary critic Jamal Mahjoub, described himself as a Sudanese of Nubian origin who thought, spoke, and wrote in English. He had left Sudan with his family in the 1980s: a period that witnessed reversals, as he recounted, of everything his parents' generation had worked for. The symposium organizers framed Gaitano and Mahjoub as representatives of a cultural present. If we take this proposition seriously, then, the "present" is no longer located almost exclusively in Khartoum; it exists in Juba as well as the many capitals of the Diaspora, not least Sharjah, where a number of Sudanese intellectuals of the 1960s–70s generation held important posts in the cultural sector. The present is also critical of the role "identity" has played thus far in shaping cultural discourse and practice and unwilling to overlook the inconsistencies and violence inherent in its binary logic.

Following the final remarks, all the participants got up on stage for a photo op. For a moment, the debate subsided. The audience rose appreciatively to its feet and clapped away. It felt like a curtain call for Sudan's compelling, if contested, "modern" past and a salute to those shaping its present outside the lines prescribed for it by state institutions.

Clare Davies received a PhD from the Institute of Fine Arts, New York University in 2014 for a dissertation entitled *Modern Egyptian Art: Site, Commodity, Archive, 1891–1948*. She was the recipient of the inaugural Irmgard Coninx Prize in Transregional Studies 2014/2015, Forum Transregionale Studien, Berlin, and is now Assistant Curator of Middle Eastern, North African, and Turkish Art at the Metropolitan Museum of Art, New York.

# Watercolor Abstracts from the Age of Empire

*By Patrick Mudekereza*
*Thursday, December 24, 2015*

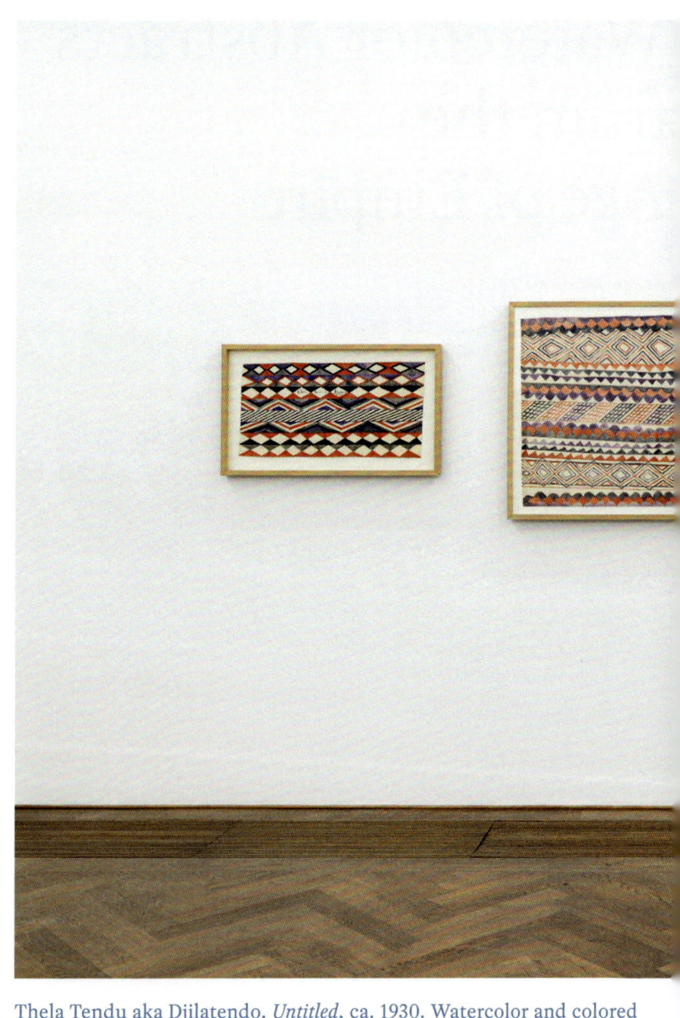

Thela Tendu aka Djilatendo, *Untitled*, ca. 1930. Watercolor and colored inks on paper; tshela-tenduo, *Untitled*, 1931. Watercolor and colored inks on paper. Both courtesy Royal Library of Belgium, Brussels. Photo: Philipp Hänger

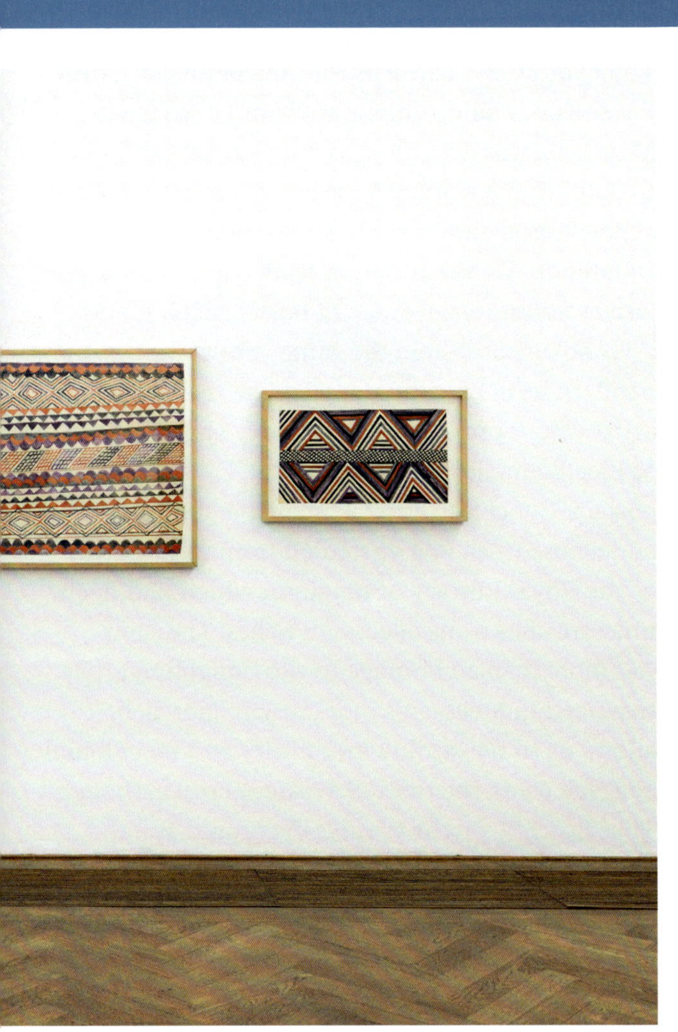

The exhibition "Patterns for (Re)cognition" at the
Basel Kunsthalle, which ran from February to
May 2015, was described as "the largest exhibition
to date" of the work of Vincent Meessen, but also
as the largest show yet of the abstract artwork of
Djilatendo. If the exhibition leaflet spares no super-
latives about its coverage of both artists, it still
does not accord them the same status. On the one
hand, there is Vincent Meessen, the rising Belgian
artist who represented his country at the 56th
Venice Biennale and, on the other, Djilatendo, an
obscure Congolese artist who died in the late 1950s
and whose work was dusted off from the archives
of the Royal Library of Belgium, which had been
unaware of its own collection's riches. The show
was more than an homage to the Congolese artist.
Inscribed in Meessen's more recent approach, it
allows us to reexamine modernity and its colonial
baggage using the tools of Western critical thought.
That last line ought to raise eyebrows. What
response, exactly, is opened up by examining the
problem of colonial denial once again in another
time, another context, but always with Western
conceptual tools?

The exhibition was built around watercolors by
Djilatendo, who is seen as one of the forerunners
of modern Congolese art, along with Albert Lubaki
and lesser-known figures such as Massalai and

Ngoma. Together, they formed the group known as the "illustrators of the Congo," which Europe "discovered" in the late 1920s by way of Georges Thiry (a colonial officer in the Belgian Congo) and Gaston-Denys Périer (an official in the colonial administration in Belgium). From 1929 to 1936, they put on exhibitions in Geneva (Geneva Ethnography Museum), Brussels (the "First National Salon of Negro Art" and an exhibition of popular art at the Royal Museums of Fine Arts), Anvers, Rome (Exhibition of Colonial Art), and Paris. Their watercolors, inspired by the practice of painting on huts, were produced on Thiry's orders and dispatched, without fail, to Europe. They only encountered qualified success upon arrival.

Djilatendo was a tailor living in Ibanc, a locality near the current city of Kananga, located in Lulua province at the center of the Democratic Republic of Congo. His work included paintings of figurative scenes illustrating his vision of modernity (cars, airplanes, characters in European dress carrying umbrellas, etc.), but also abstract watercolors. He illustrated the book *L'éléphant qui marchait sur les œufs* (The Elephant Who Walked on Eggs), the first publication of folktales transcribed by a Congolese author named Badibanga.

In "Patterns for (Re)cognition," Vincent Meessen places Djilatendo's abstract watercolors in dialogue with examinations by André Ombredane, a French psychologist who introduced cognitive tests aimed at identifying the best "ethnicities" or choosing hired hands for colonial industry. The films were made by Robert Maistriaux, to whom Meessen pays fairly little regard, apart from the credits for the video on Ombredane's Congo TAT test. Maistriaux wrote the treatise *L'intelligence noire et son destin* (Black Intelligence and Its Destiny), published in 1957—four years after the video shown at the exhibition—containing hard pronouncements about the intelligence of the groups subjected to the tests, especially those living "in the bush." We read, for example, that: "In essence, the black man's early childhood takes place in an environment intellectually inferior to anything we can imagine in Europe" (p. 191).

The tests, designed in part to measure the test-taker's ability to respond to abstract shapes, were used to demonstrate these assertions. Vincent Meessen's demonstration runs contrary to this pseudo-intellectual approach by referencing Djilatendo's abstract work from 1920 to 1940. In an interview from July 22, 2015, Meessen explained: "Seeing how this connection to intelligence was drawn, one cannot help connecting it to abstract art that was produced at the same time and had an incredible boom in Europe."

Imagine how conflicting it can be for young Black Brazilians to form their identity while growing up surrounded by mostly negative references to Blackness.

Thiago de Paula Souza, academic, curator

Meessen is also interested in the transition from painting on huts to painting on paper and the introduction of the signature, which marks the birth of the artist as an individual and speaks to a production opening up to the art market. Djilatendo signed his work in many ways: ThselaTendu, tshelatendu, tshe latendu, Tshela tendu, Thelatedu, tshielatendu, thielatedo, Tshalo Ntende, and so on. Based on work by the German scholar Katherin Langenhol, Meessen counted a total of forty-two spellings of Djilatendo. He was likewise interested in the signature's placement on the painting and notes that the artist attempts to repeat a motif until he reaches a transformative shape—which is where he signs his own name in one of its manifold spellings. Elsewhere in the same interview, Meesen said: "He is ordered to ensure the artwork's authenticity. It is my firm belief that he is making a conscious gesture, playing with the colonial criterion of fixity as a trait of the modern artist. And even if he did not do so consciously, the artist was at times foiling the alphabet, the tool of identification imposed on him, and the ensuing fixity. Thus he enabled himself to travel in his work."

With the two iterations of the exhibition, Meessen changed the name of the artist with whom he was co-exhibiting. At the Kiosk in Gent, it was Tshiela

Ntendu. At the Kunstalle in Basel, it is Thela Tendu.
It seems to me that in renouncing the more or less
established spelling of Djilatendo and in modifying
the name in the exhibition's publicity, he is diluting
the artist's identity when in fact the artist intended
to multiply it.

In addition, the Swiss version of the exhibition,
which distributes around thirty watercolors among
five rooms, never entirely devotes the space to the
expression of Djilatendo, who is invariably subju-
gated to other voices, all of them Western. The first
room places them in dialogue with the films about
Ombredane's tests. The second highlights their
commonalities with the paintings of Paul Klee and
their Kuba identity. The third returns to Ombredane's
publications. The fourth is devoted to revisiting
Jan Vansina, the patriarch of oral history who met
Djilatendo in 1953. In the fifth room, Meessen
opted to exhibit his own work, covering the entire
floor and creating dialogue with the space. It is as
if, in order to find its place in modernity, this
Congolese voice needs Western "backing" or interpretation, endorsing its place in the hallowed halls.

I note with satisfaction the varying approach
taken by the following project, "Personnes et les
autres" (Persons and Others), presented at the
Venice Biennale. There, Vincent Meessen shares

an encounter with Joseph M'Belolo Ya M'Piku, a
Congolese member of the Situationist International,
and brings to life a text he composed in May 1968.

All of this reminds us of the great task that remains
before us: to rewrite the history, the histories, of art
or thought, according to the perspectives of colonized
peoples. Meessen reminds us of the necessity of
profound, ongoing work of rethinking, rewriting, and,
to paraphrase V. Y. Mudimbe, *reprendre*.

Patrick Mudekereza is a writer and cultural producer, living and
working in Lubumbashi, DRC. He runs the WAZA art center,
and co-founded Rencontres Picha, the Biennale of Lubumbashi.

# A Fragile City
# Built on Sand

*A conversation between Youssef Limoud and Elsa Guily*
*Monday, May 23, 2016*

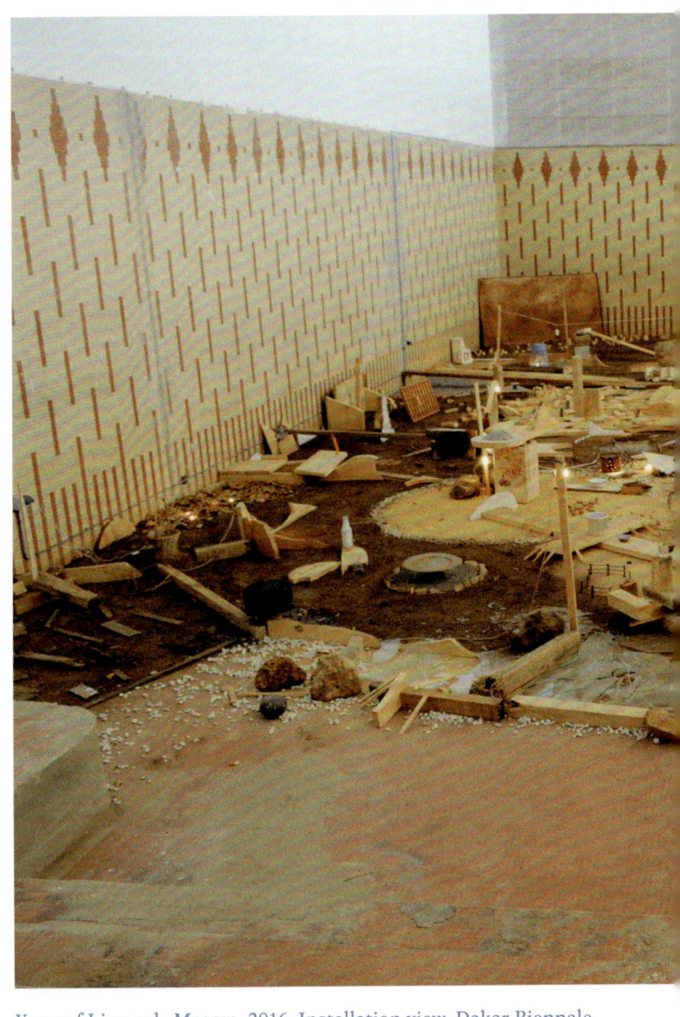

Youssef Limoud, *Maqam*, 2016. Installation view, Dakar Biennale. Courtesy of the artist

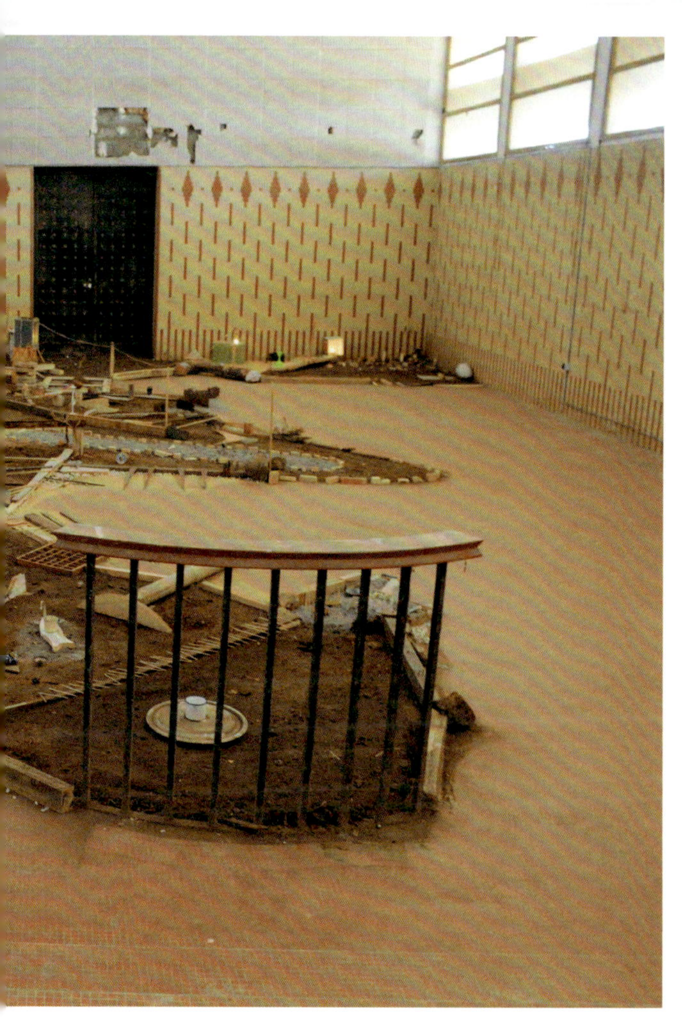

The Leopold Senghor award at Dak'art 2016 was given
to the Egyptian-Swiss artist Youssef Limoud for
his work *Maqam*, installed in the former court of
the Palais de Justice. The installation was serene,
recalling the calm after a storm. It gave shape to the
viewer's imagination of what *The City in the Blue
Daylight*—a line from a poem by Senghor and Simon
Njami's theme for the biennial—could be.

"An artist has to be a visionary. Someone who
sees things without looking but by sensing their
materiality," says the artist. "*Maqam* is an installation
in progress, happening in different chapters and
places. I started working on this idea of the city
three years ago in reaction to the pictures of
destruction happening in Syria. The notion of ruins
taps into my own sensitivity—it raises questions
about socio-political circumstances while speaking
about geological facts and the passage of time.
We are living in a chaotic world in constant motion.

"For the Dakar Biennale, the most important
aspect of this installation was the encounter with
the space itself. I had to integrate the space into the
work, to avoid a separation between site and work.
As such I incorporated the witness stand and other
aspects of the place into the work of art. While
I started by using whatever materials left around in
the Palais de Justice that attracted me, I also let
myself be influenced by the city of Dakar, in which I

saw the simultaneous existence of a precarious state of things, as well as something very fine. This city might be under ongoing construction, but people still live in a kind of harmony. Behind the rough and tough materiality, you feel this passion and the finesse of things. Through the precarious aspect of my work, I wanted to reflect on this fragility of the world.

"I had to make the work in three days, which meant that the objects used in the work were collected and chosen within the process of creating the work. The artistic process in this installation, as well as in my paintings, is based on the principle of collage and collecting. The objects collected signify the motion of living: each thing was once inhabited with our presence and are now traces of a fragmented life, bringing a poetic aspect to the work. Assembling this work was an endless search—conscious and unconscious—for relations and encounters between things. When I do a work of art there is always a geometrical aspect that comes out, like a calculation that underlines the relations be-tween the elements of the work. Here, I wanted the viewer to step into the work in order to emphasize the tension between the different elements, as well as the huge scale of the installation. I installed a lamp in order to light the city at the end of day, to give it life. If you are here around seven, when day is changing into night, you may feel this change from light to dark with these small lamps.

"The night before the opening I was still working on the installation, but sometimes it is inspiring to do things in a hurry.  Anticipating every element of the work may kill creative feelings. I work primarily with intuition. If I have to find a solution for a work, I cover my head in bed—even if I'm not sleeping—and dream a solution. In this act of lying down one can meditate and many of my previous works have happened like this. The act of doing may take a short or long time.

"The narrative aspects of the work is present in the objects themselves, but it is also emphasized in the title *Maqam*, which has many meanings in Arabic. The first one is home, the place where one feels comfortable, but tinged with  a sense of nostalgia. Another reading could refer to a shrine where sacred people are buried and where one goes to worship and to be blessed; in other words, the notion of death is also present in the work. The third meaning has to do with Arabic music scales. This narrative element in the work is also underlined by the use of sand and soil, embodying the earth, one of the four elements in ancient Indian philosophy. Light is non-material and, used together with soil, it creates a sensitive fluidity in the work.

127

"*Maqam* is not a maquette, representing an idea
of the city: it is above all a poetic statement, which
I visualize using found materials full of aesthetic
qualities. It is about breathing a vision through the
materiality of the city. It can also be read as a direct
response to Simon Njami's concept 'The City in
the Blue Daylight' because in my work, in the Palais
de Justice, you feel as if you were walking through
the city of Dakar. I am curious to learn what people
see in it, because they add something to the work
through interpreting it. Njami has managed to break
this line between art and life by choosing works
that engage with this concept. Choosing the Palais
de Justice as a site of art reappropriates this
neglected place of history and thereby reshapes the
confusing narratives embedded in these walls.

"The power of the biennale is this idea of engaging
the past in order to reshape or re-enchant our
present. *Maqam* may evoke criticism for modernist
architecture, as well as the civilizing project of
modernity that now seems very fragile and ephemeral. If modernity seems inevitable because of the
spread of capitalism, works of art can at least
critique this vision of the world. Art should stand
against the corruption of the mind and should
improve our critical vision of the world. It is all
about consciousness. You can make beautiful
things but, without consciousness, you are missing

128

the point of doing things. I agree with Nietzsche that art makes life meaningful. I see art as a spiritual and meditative way to speak about what I feel, in order to give meaning to life. That is why I believe in art!"

Elsa Guily is an art historian and an independent art critic living in Berlin, looking at the intersection between decolonial practices, critical theory, and visual representations. In addition, she works as an Assistant Editor for *Contemporary And*.

# When I was at school, I hated art and gave it up as early as I could.

Emma Wolukau-Wanambwa, artist

# Searching for New Forms in Old Rituals

*A conversation between Senga Nengudi
and Naomi Beckwith*
*Wednesday, March 27, 2013*

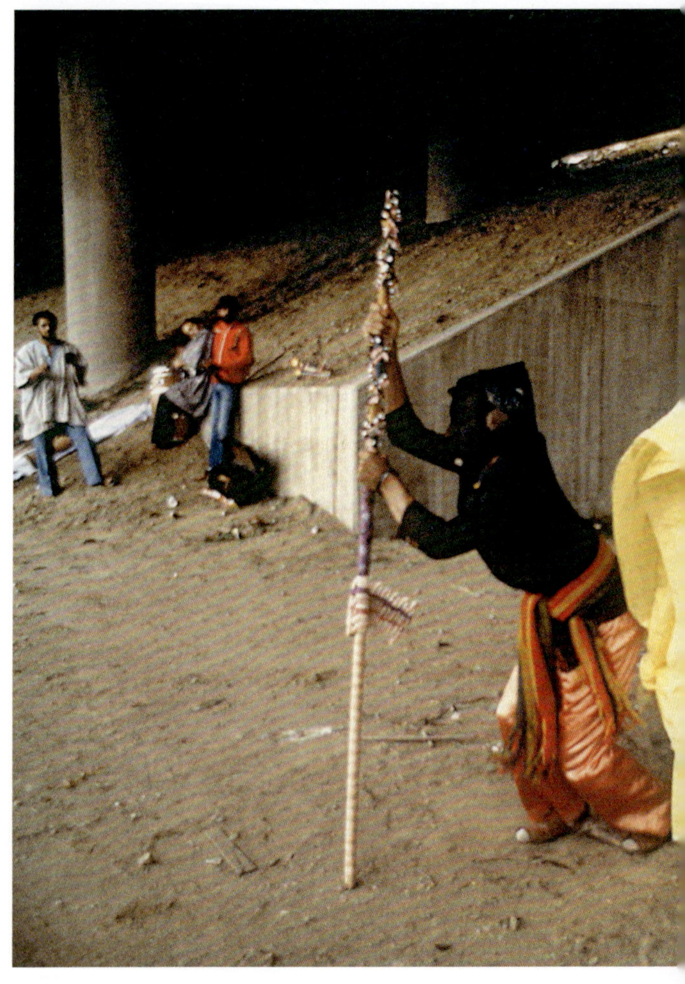

Senga Nengudi, *Ceremony for Freeway Fets*, 1978. Performance in collaboration with David Hammons, Maren Hassinger, and Studio Z members,
Los Angeles. Courtesy of the artist and Thomas Erben Gallery

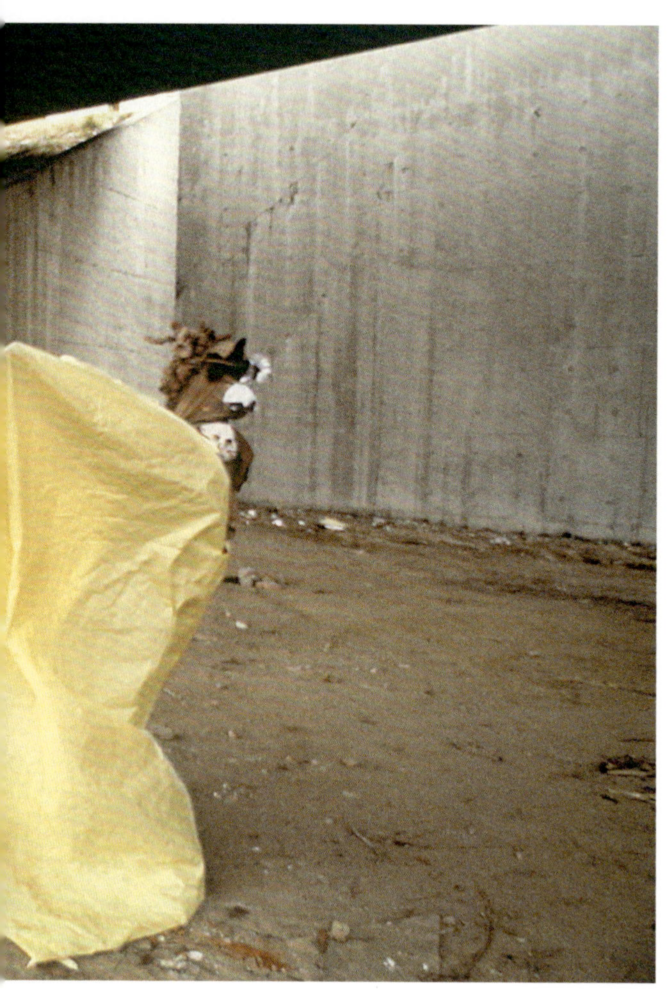

The American artist Senga Nengudi, born in 1943, is renowned for her performance-based sculptures and installations exploring aspects of the human body in relation to ritual, philosophy, and spirituality. Nengudi is regarded as a core member of the African-American avant-garde—with artists such as David Hammons and Maren Hassinger—as it was concentrated in Los Angeles during the 1970s and early 1980s.

*Naomi Beckwith:* I'd like to start our conversation from your recent work, so that we'll trace our way back. You just mounted the show "Lov u"—what inspired that?

*Senga Nengudi:* Well, I have this kind of voyeuristic way of overhearing snippets of conversations (like when I'm on the New York subway). When people talk, when you get off the phone, for instance, it always ends in: "love you." And this phrase isn't obligatory, it comes from a real place. From there I started thinking of the people I love and examining true love. I started gathering definitions from friends about what love means to them. I worked with students, I created a photo book, I got the local community involved, and had them and the students take pictures with things they love. People were pleased to have to think about love and not just in a romantic way. And that's what I wanted: the exhibition to be a place for conversation about how love functions in your life. I also wanted to use materials like masking tape. I work with the materials and then figure out the message as I finish. Some people accuse me of being too cerebral, but I was just doing things, making my art, and realized many people I feel deeply about were no longer on this plane but are symbolically represented in this work, they are always with me.

*Beckwith:* It's also a very multimedia work.

*Nengudi:* I knew I wanted it to be multimedia work but it had to be a low-tech multimedia. Things that were available felt right for the situation. I also wanted a soundtrack, to go along with the visual, putting you in the mood, so to speak. Some of the sounds are very abstract like Cecil Taylor, and some literal music, like Nancy Wilson and Isaac Hayes. I noticed that there's rarely any sound in galleries, but in our community there's always sounds. In Cuba music is everywhere; in Harlem that's true too. I could not tolerate the idea of not having sound in the show. At the last hour of the last day of the show, I changed the soundtrack to an "om" chant—it was a way of clearing the energy and purifying the space.

*Beckwith:* You also recently re-performed *RSVP* at Contemporary Art Museum Houston—how was that for you?

*Nengudi:* Very difficult. My pieces are fairly simple so you would think it would be easier, but obviously

I'm not in that same space. I do find that *RSVP* still has legs because some of the issues it dealt with are more intense now than when the work originated. It  was about things related to feminist issues, to a sense of body, how body issues related to self-esteem and self-acceptance. It was also about entanglements—being entangled by your stuff and stretching yourself beyond your limits. Having that sense of elasticity is still very important, and that I use the same materials. No one really wears pantyhose anymore, but people still read them as being about restriction. I was pleased at the emotional responses at CAMH, especially from women who said that they felt like their story was being told. Those comments were very special to me.

*Beckwith: RSVP* was visionary in that it was an ephemeral performance and it made an object—did you think of that consciously at the time?

*Nengudi:* You know, people talk about Richard Pryor and how his comedy was true stuff: whatever he was feeling, he gave to the audience with no buffer. In a sense, this was me laying my guts on the line. I was going through a lot of stress and wanting to express it. I was experimenting with materials like resin and glue, and I didn't know where this was going but I had to try it. I knew I had three interests: working with material, working with space, and working with emotions. And I always get back to a relationship to the body. When I was growing up in L.A., there was this place downtown called Clifton's Cafeteria. The owner may have been religious because there would be these little nooks and crannies that look like Roman catacombs or grottoes on each floor of the café. I'll never forget this: you had to go down to the basement for the bathroom and at the bottom of the stairs was a giant Jesus statue and you could sit on his lap! I related to that. When I want to be a sculptor, I want people to touch things.

*Beckwith:* You don't just want to make an object in space but an object with a relation to the viewer's body.

*Nengudi:* Yes, I was in a dance class where we were told to hug ourselves. I realize that we go through the world without touching ourselves or others.

*Beckwith:* It seems these objects aren't really abstract; they are about a body's relationship to another which can be very political.

*Nengudi:* Exactly. These objects were related to performance and also to rituals that define these relationships.

*Beckwith:* Such as?

*Nengudi:* When I worked with dance, I was interested in basic movement issues such as: how is this guy going to lift me? At the same time, I was also at the Watts Towers Arts Center and the Pasadena Arts Museum, which were both very

138

experimental. There were Happenings, and [Claes] Oldenburg and [Robert] Rauschenberg came to visit. In those places, I could move how I wanted to move, do what I wanted to do visually. Then I went to Japan, where I sought out Gutai. In Japan there is a ritual for everything—even for how you talk on the phone—and you can't veer off from that or it becomes something different. And I thought: how does this involve my own culture? How does this look like African culture? All these elements blended into my performance practice, but I wasn't aware of it until much later on. It wasn't until I started thinking about Dada that I realized that even way before Dada, way before our people hit the shores of America, there was ritual, improvisation, and per-formance, but in America, it was about survival as a way of getting through the day. Our African-American history was about how the way we are in the world is already a performance, where sometimes even the way we use language has a double meaning.

*Beckwith:* Your most famous public performance is *Ceremony for Freeway Fets* (in collaboration with David Hammons, Maren Hassinger, and Studio Z members). How did you develop it?

*Nengudi:* There was just this particular energy in L.A. at the time and the home gallery was Brockman run by Alonzo Davis with Suzanne Jackson as project coordinator. Many Black artists there were very interested in Sun Ra. We loosely formed this collective called Studio Z where we worked together, played together. Everyone was generous to come together to do this thing. It was African and Kabuki-like at the same time. I wanted to link the two things that seemed to have nothing in common and the linkage was the importance of ritual. In Japanese and African culture, like oral history, things have to be very specific. It also had to be a total experience—it incorporated all elements like dance, music; it involved costumes. Again, there was no separation between forms, all of it worked together.

*Beckwith:* How did you choreograph it?

*Nengudi:* It was 100% improvisation. I created the costumes, though David [Hammons] made his own stuff, and I created a public artwork as the setting. The performance was the opening ceremony, the consecration of the public artwork and space. The 1970s were such a difficult time for male/female relationships in the black community. So I brought these elements together and I was the spirit that united the male and female. It was a healing. I also created these masks out of pantyhose—I had never really had the masked experience before. But when I put on the mask, I totally became another entity and I began to understand these ritual forms: once you put that mask on you become an agent of something else.

*Beckwith:* There was a lot of general interest in Africa at this time. How did you personally conceive of Africa?

*Nengudi:* When I was in college there was barely any instruction on African art, though I had been interested in it since high school. I took French because every time I did research, I found that the only books of any consequence were in French. But it brought tears to my eyes to read the awful way they wrote about the people. I once visited the Museum of Man in France and saw the body of Saartje Baartman. I thought: how could they do that to a human being? Put them in a case like that?

Then one day—long after that—I was in the kitchen and I heard something on the TV—there was a lot of talking. It sounded like New York and I turned toward the TV and it was African people! They had the same tone and rhythm that I've heard on 125th Street. Anywhere in this world, the Diaspora is. You don't even have to work at it, it manifests itself in you. When I looked at books and museums, I found "their" view of us but I did not find the truth. I found the real deal in myself. The real deal is looking at the old traditional African dance and dance on any diasporic city street and see the new that looks like the old.

# Our major issue was the labeling of Black artists' work.

David Koloane, artist, educator, facilitator, and curator

Naomi Beckwith is a curator at the Museum of Contemporary Art, Chicago. She was previously the Associate Curator at the Studio Museum in Harlem. Beckwith holds an MA with Distinction from the Courtauld Institute of Art in London and was a Critical Studies Fellow at the Whitney Museum Independent Study Program.

# I Feel More Like a Health Practitioner

*A conversation between Tabita Rezaire and*
*An Paenhuysen*
*Tuesday, July 5, 2016*

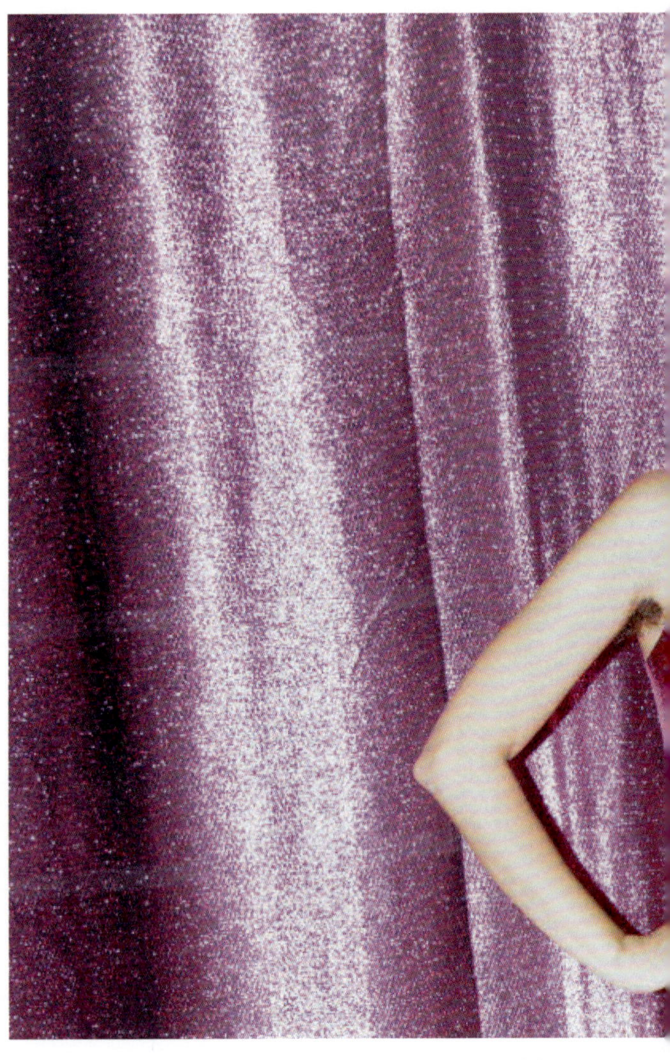

Tabita Rezaire, *Portrait from Cunty Party*, 2016. Courtesy of the artist

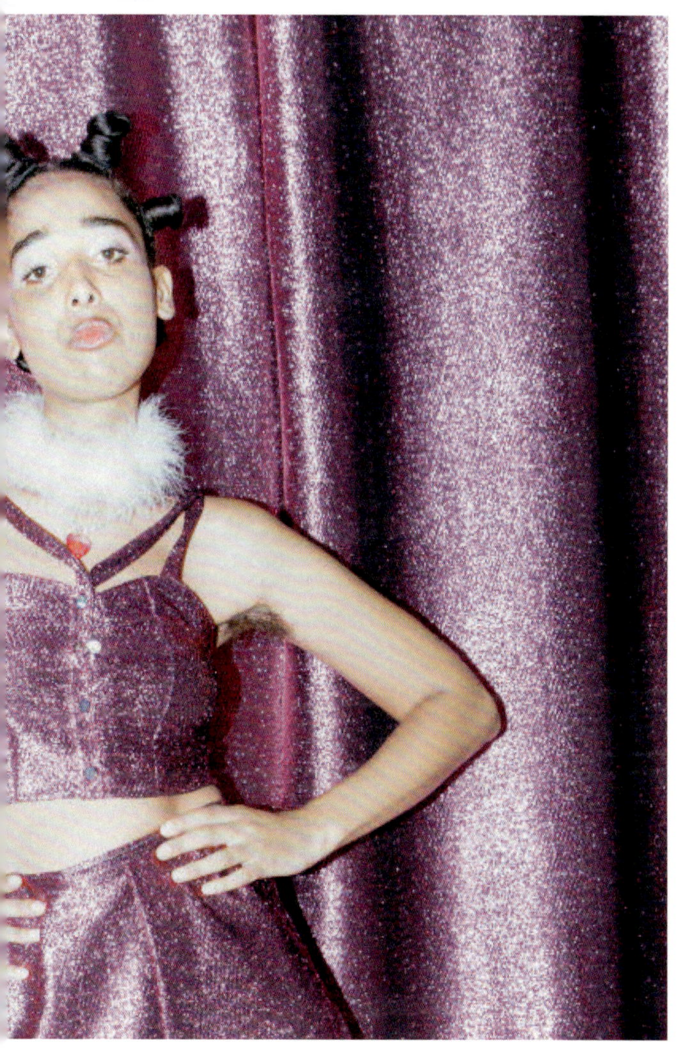

*An Paenhuysen:* You call yourself a "warrior-healer." Could you tell us a little about the wounds you're healing with your art?

*Tabita Rezaire:* Survival hurts—for every conscious being. Yet for some it's harder as the society they live in devaluates their existence or consistently persecutes their lives. Internalized and accumulated pains from generational, ancestral, or experienced traumas make one's ability to navigate the world a struggle. These traumas may manifest in different ways, but I believe they all stem from severe disconnections. We are disconnected from the earth, from each other, from our own selves, and from the universe. A warrior-healer is seeking to restore energetic balance on all those levels. Because fighting alone is consuming and draining, if you don't have tools to nurture your energies you'll burn out.

*An Paenhuysen:* The mind-spirit-body pollution inflicted through white Western dominance is a topic in your work on all levels: from visual language to food. Yet your major focus and tool is the Internet. Why?

*Tabita Rezaire:* Well it isn't, I just get asked about this more. All realms of our realities need to be decolonized. Because it is our health that needs to be politicized. And our health is equally threatened by our diet, the shaming of our cultures, the fetishization of our bodies, the murders of our siblings, and the technologies that we use. I don't impose a hierarchy on what needs to be dismantled. It is the whole colonial-capitalist-patriarchal-scientific-technological-medical-penal-educational complex that needs to be taken down. For this to happen, we need to re-connect and decolonize on all levels and become response-able. That is a commitment and a long journey: healing takes time. Healing is hard. Healing hurts. And it is not linear. We'll collapse again and again, but each time we'll be able to deal better with what's to come.

*An Paenhuysen:* Your video work suggests the idea of "unlearning" the Internet. That's a difficult thing to do, because once one has learned the rules, they become invisible. How do you go about it?

*Tabita Rezaire:* Like any institutionalized violence, the Internet is pervasive and insidious, especially when you benefit from it. That's why we're complicit. Because even if it is a coercive, exploitative, and oppressive space, it's cool. I guess it comes down to how much we're willing to compromise.

In practical terms I feel like there are two strategies. One is about occupying and creating safer spaces within a violent system, by being vocal and providing counter-representations and counter-narratives. In doing that though, you are still being complicit in an exploitative and oppressive structure.

The other strategy is about dismantling and re-creating a more sustainable, safe, and fair information and communication technology. That's the real vision: rejecting the actual system although you're benefiting from it. Technically I'm not sure what that would mean in Internet terms, maybe encrypted P2P networks, or, to a certain extent, using the deep web. But I'm confident that something will manifest.

*An Paenhuysen:* Internet aesthetics are not always the most attractive. Yet how important is beauty in your work for you?

*Tabita Rezaire:* Beauty is not really something I think of in terms of my work. I wouldn't be able to define what I find beautiful or what beauty means. Although I know it is very important to me, more in terms of the space I inhabit or the people I surround myself with—in the sense of a radiant energy.

I wonder why you don't find Internet aesthetics attractive. According to which standards? What resonates within each of us is all very subjective and constructed, especially in terms of art appreciation. For me, it's more about the ability to feel uplifted, divine, and grateful for what I've witnessed or manifested. Beauty is about raising our vibrational frequency and that's what healing is.

*An Paenhuysen:* You're an activist—you're an artist. I'm confused. I thought those were two separate things. How do you see it?

*Tabita Rezaire:* Well, you can be or do many different things simultaneously. You can be a lawyer

# Focusing on alternative forms and maneuvers does not mean escaping from the present status quo.

Julia Grosse and Yvette Mutumba, art historians, *C&* founders and editors-in-chief and a porn star. The legacy of modernity and its oppressive logic of rationality deny what life is about: interconnection, paradox, and contradiction. The obsession with one-dimensional specialization is also dangerous because it develops a culture of arrogant ignorance. Artist and activist are just de-nominations among many that could apply. As I've said before, I feel more like a health practitioner providing and sharing tools to nurture our emotional, political, technological, and spiritual health. So my work as an artist, researcher, yoga teacher, community worker, emotional laborer, cosmetics maker, gardener, friend, and lover seeks to convey and share my vision.

*An Paenhuysen:* Does art have healing powers? Is it spiritual?

*Tabita Rezaire:* Art can have the power to heal. Everything holds the potential to heal or hurt, depending on uses and users. So art can heal but it can also be a tool of repression and coercion. There are countless examples of art being used as a tool for dangerous propaganda. Now, is art spiritual? That is where art comes from. Before there was an art market tied to an unregulated capitalist financial system, art was a medium for connecting with a higher power. Communities worldwide used artistic forms to communicate, praise, receive, and give thanks to the divine. Here again, we've been disconnected from our purpose. Now we are creating commodities to be consumed and sold. I don't think art has lost its power, though.

*An Paenhuysen:* Are you ever afraid of your artwork being perceived as "esoteric"?

*Tabita Rezaire:* Why should I be afraid? There will always be people who resonate with who I am and what I do and others who won't, and that's fine. Society lives off our self-doubts and feeds off our fears. I have no time for that. I am comfortable that what I create comes from a place of love, and as Alexandra Kelbert so beautifully put it: "I rage out of love and I love in rage."

*An Paenhuysen:* The Western art market has Africa on its radar at the moment. What is your take on this trend?

*Tabita Rezaire:* Well, the art market is just Columbusing, busy "discovering" new territories, new resources and capital to accumulate. It has positive effects though: it challenges the monolithic landscape of art, and gives economic opportunities to more artists to have their works shown and sold. Unfortunately many African countries do not invest enough in the arts, so there is less of a culture of "collectors." What happens is that most artworks made by African artists get sold to Western collectors or institutions. Which is sad because once again it is cultural capital leaving the continent. We have to be vigilant that "African art" doesn't only reflect a romanticized construction that caters to a Western audience. I, for certain, am also benefiting from this  sudden interest. Some may feel, inappropriately, as I've lived in South Africa for less than two years. But then, isn't the Pan-African project to encompass all diasporic identities?

*An Paenhuysen:* You've started the tech health company NTU, you run the art studio Malaxa, and you're launching another new space. What is the benefit of collaboration for you?

*Tabita Rezaire:* There's this cheesy meme that's been circulating a lot: "if you wanna go fast, go alone, if you wanna go far, go together." But truly: collaboration is so powerful it creates magic. It's about joining forces and I'm blessed to be able to work with people I love and admire. Also showcasing other people's work and vision is very important for me, because I don't exist in a vacuum. Building a network of people that acknowledge and promote each other's worth is vital. Especially within the art world, which is all about ego and competition.

An Paenhuysen works as a freelance curator, art critic, and educator living in Berlin. She is a fervent art blogger and teaches art criticism online at the Node Center for Curatorial Studies.

# A Short History of Decolonialism and Delinking

*A conversation between Walter Mignolo and Aïcha Diallo*
*Thursday, August 7, 2014*

*Aïcha Diallo:* Decolonial aesthetics is a concept
you have developed in the process of your reflections
and work. How did this come about?

*Walter Mignolo:* First of all, this notion, like any
concept of the modernity/coloniality/decoloniality
collective project, is a consequence of collective
conversations. It was introduced in the conversation
by Adolfo Alban Achinte, perhaps toward 2003,
when he was still a PhD candidate at the Universidad
Andina Simón Bolívar in Quito, Ecuador. It came
out of conversations on the colonial matrix of power:
what is the place of aesthetics in the colonial matrix?
We have been talking about coloniality of knowledge
and coloniality of being, political and economic
coloniality, or coloniality of religion trapping spirituality, coloniality of gender and sexuality, coloniality
of ethnicity (from which racism sprung). But we
had not yet touched aesthetics. And the reason was
that none of us up to that point were artists or art
historians or art critics. But Adolfo was, being an
artist and activist, from the Colombian Pacific,
Afro-Colombian.

It was in the summer of 2009 that the issue
exploded. At that point Adolfo was already the
assistant to the director of the program, Catherine
Walsh. I have been a professor and collaborator
of Catherine Walsh since the beginning of the PhD
program. Pedro Pablo Gómez, from the School of

Fine Arts in Bogotá, was working on his PhD but
was also the general editor of a new publication,
*CALLE 14. revista de investigacion en el campo del arte*
(STREET 14. Journal of investigation in the field
of art). He invited me to write an article for the journal.
The article "Aesthesis Decolonial" was published
in March of 2010. But while the article was in production (I finished it in the fall of 2009) Pedro Pablo
suggested to co-curate an exhibit-cum-workshop
with the title "Estéticas Descoloniales" (Decolonial
Aesthetics). The subtitle became, in the process,
"Sentir, pensar y hacer en Abya-Yala" (Sensing,
thinking, and doing in Abya Yala). We emphasized
"sensing, thinking, and doing," breaking away from
the European eighteenth-century distinction
and hierarchy between "knowing, rationality" and
"sensing, emotions." Meanwhile, Adolfo was in
Argentina participating in a workshop organized by
Zulma Palermo, in Salta, a member of the collective.
Zulma was also working with some of her colleagues
and students on the question of an aesthetics/aesthe-
sis.

What is crucial to keep in mind is that "coloniality" and all the concepts we have introduced since
then are concepts whose point of origination is not
in Europe but in "the Third World." That means
that all these concepts emerge from the experience of
coloniality in the Americas. Entangled with modernity

to be sure, but no longer "applying" European-born categories to "understand" colonial legacies. On the contrary, we have converted Europe into a domain of analysis rather than a provider of "cultural and epistemic resources."

*Aïcha Diallo:* In terms of looking closer at its foundations, to which movements and thinkers in the past can this concept be traced back? What are the actual points of origin, specifically when contextualized in Africa and in the Diasporas?

*Walter Mignolo:* Thanks for this question that allows me to reinforce my last point. The historical foundations are not to be searched for in Europe. The profuse use of "decolonization" is remarkable after World War II, with the processes of decolonization in Asia and Africa. However, the institutional turning point for me was the Bandung Conference of 1955. It was, to be sure, a state-oriented and state-managed conference. But the message was clear: neither capitalism nor communism but decolonization. And the first sentence of Sukarno's inaugural speech was, more or less, "this is the first time in the history of humankind that an international conference of people of color is taking place." As it is known, twenty-nine Asian and African states attended, including China, which was under Mao and certainly in a somewhat uncomfortable situation. "People of color" meant also people of non-Christian religions. States with a majority or significant Muslim population had a significant presence at the conference. Now, these principles were somewhat denaturalized when Bandung mutated into "non-aligned countries," whose first meeting was in Belgrade, under Marshal Tito, in 1961.

Now, since Bandung and the struggle for decolonization in Asia and Africa, during the Cold War, and the works of Aimé Césaire and Frantz Fanon, mainly, the concept of "decolonization" has gained currency, and it is today used in different projects from decolonizing religion and gender/sexuality, to decolonizing the state and the economy, to decolonizing aesthetics and scholarship, knowledge, and subjectivity, the academy, the university, etc.

*Aïcha Diallo:* In this respect, how would you define Fanon's legacies analyzing the "coloniality of power" as a point of reference?

*Walter Mignolo:* Fanon's legacy is and has been crucial for "decoloniality" at large. And more specific in our project, the work of Nelson Maldonado-Torres at the intersection of Fanonian legacies and the decolonial project of the collective I mentioned have already made two crucial moves: one is the anatomy of "coloniality of being," and the other is to move from Levinas's intervention in continental philosophy through his Jewish experience and knowledge, to Dussel (an Argentine of German descent and founder of philosophy of liberation, where he confronts Levinas based on the local and colonial histories of the Americas) and finally to Fanon. This doesn't mean that we, in the collective, are the owners of Fanon. There are many others who take on Fanon's decolonial legacies, and all are welcomed. I would highlight, however, the project of the Caribbean Philosophical Association, founded by Jamaican philosopher Lewis Gordon. I mention this because there has been since its inception a fruitful, extensive, and convivial conversation between modernity/coloniality and the Philosophical Association. We share the lived experiences (yes I know, experiences are "constructed," which doesn't mean that they are not "lived experiences") of continental South and Central America and the Caribbean. The anchors of those experiences differ and at the same time are complementary. For Afro-Caribbeans, the anchors are the histories of the Middle Passage. For us, in the collective modernity/coloniality, it is the histories of our European ancestors (Spaniards, Portuguese, Dutch, French, British, Germans) who invaded, appropriated, and expropriated the land and made themselves at home, disregarding the native population and the great civilizations of the "New World," and committed one of the largest crimes of humanity by hunting down and enslaving people from Africa.

Djilatendo signed
his work in many ways:
Thsela Tendu,
Tshelatendu,
tshe latendz,
Tshela tendu,
Thelatedu,
tshielatendu,
thielatedo,
Tshal Ntende,
etc.

Patrick Mudekereza, writer and cultural operator

*Aïcha Diallo:* Can you elaborate on the term "delinking" that you coined?

*Walter Mignolo:* First of all, I did not coin "delinking." It was the Egyptian Marxist sociologist Samir Amin, who introduced it in 1982 in a book published in Paris. The title was *La déconnexion*, translated into English as "delinking." Amin's proposal was to delink from capitalism, that is, he argued for an economic delinking.

What I did was to re-cast the term to talk about "delinking from the colonial matrix of power," which is larger than delinking from capitalism. And delinking not to socialism but to transmodernity and pluriversality, where there is no room for any abstract universal. So socialism is an option, as are many others looking to delink from the frame of mind we are in today, but cannot be the option, that is, the only way "to delink to." In the process of sorting out and delinking from the two options derived from the European Enlightenment, either (neo-)liberalism or (neo-)socialism, I came to understand the current world order in terms of re-Westernization, de-Westernization, and decoloniality.

*Aïcha Diallo:* In light of decoloniality, to what extent could you say that the biennale as such is a structure that generally carries the basis of hegemonic knowledge systems, i.e. by creating some forms of exclusion along the lines of gender, border, and migration? In this context how do you perceive Dak'Art, the biennale in Dakar that focuses on artists and artistic productions from the continent —including sub-Saharan and North Africa and the Diasporas?

*Walter Mignolo:* There are two directions or options in which delinking (or *détournement*) is taking place in the sphere of art, museums, biennials, or triennials. The question consists of "reading" the project that propels and motivates the events or the enactment of archives (e.g., museums). One is de-Westernization. I have already written some pieces on this, apropos of the Sharjah Biennial 11, the Museum of Islamic Art in Doha, and the Asian Civilizations Museum in Singapore.

Dak'Art is for me more difficult to read. On the one hand, it started clearly inscribed in the philosophy and sensibility of African variegated processes of decolonization. It seems to me Dak'Art is halfway between the legacies of European modernity and the history of decolonization in Africa. What makes the de-Westernization of the Sharjah Biennial radical, for instance, is that it is supported by financial capital. And here is the catch-22 that makes "cultural" de-Westernization difficult to understand: it is "thanks" to impressive economic growth that cultural de-Westernization is possible. And it is the lack of strong financial autonomy that makes

Dak'Art navigate between the legacies of European modernity and the motivation for decolonization. Dak'Art can bring the Third World and Europe to the ex-Third World. I see Dak'Art as a site to promote and enhance Pan-Africanism in the art sphere. And Pan-Africanism could be decolonial but it may not necessarily be.

Dak'Art could run parallel to Sharjah Biennial as an institution that not only promotes and supports African artists but sets up a clear and radical project of re-emergence. That is, that re-inscribes in the cultural sphere the spirit of Bandung and the spirit of African decolonization as we find it in Amilcar Cabral, Frantz Fanon, Steve Biko, and Walter Rodney if we would like to bring the African Diaspora into the picture.

*Aïcha Diallo:* Could you name any artists and artistic productions in African as well as Afrodiasporic contexts that follow a decolonial trajectory? In which way?

*Walter Mignolo:* I have been working with Afro-diasporic artists, curators, critiques, etc. And all of them, the ones I work with, are fully engaged in decolonial talks, exhibits, workshops, and the like.

I'll mention three examples:

Patrice Naiambana, from Sierra Leone. He created Tribal Soul in 1992. He has become globally known through his spectacular tour-de-force one-man play, *The Man Who Committed Thought*. I met him in 2011 at the Middelburg Decolonial Summer School. He performed *The Man* as part of the summer school. His father was involved in the struggle for decolonization in Sierra Leone, so nothing new to him there. His storytelling (wich is how we agreed on describing what he does) is clearly decolonial. His thoughts are a continuation of his performance.

A second case is Jeannette Elhers. Born in Denmark to a Trinidian father and a Danish mother, Jeannette embodies the stories of empire and the Atlantic. Storytelling such as *Invisible Empires* (2010), where her father is the narrator, and *Atlantic* (2009–2010), where she digs into sounds and images to make sense of the horror of the slave trade, or the magnificent *Black Bullets* (2012), imagined after the Haitian Revolution, are also magnificent achievements enacting decolonial aesthetics. You can see all of this on Jeannette's web page.

A third example is the work that Alanna Lockward, an Afro-Dominican residing in Berlin, has been doing through [the film screening series and trans-disciplinary roundtable] Be.Bop: Black Europe-Body Politics, with editions in 2012, 2013, and 2014 in Berlin and Copenhagen. I bring up Alanna here because it is not just a question of artists/storytellers, whether visual, verbal, or written, dance or sounds, videos or movies, documentary or fiction; it is also about the importance of curators who have the possibility of bringing decoloniality in many strands.

But I cannot finish without mentioning *Le malentendu colonial* (2004) by Jean Marie Téno. I have been using this movie in my classes introducing decolonial thinking, doing, sensing, and believing. Decolonial aesthetics/aesthesis has become a connector across the continents.

Walter Mignolo is an Argentinian semiotician, writer, researcher, and professor at Duke University, Durham, and Director of the Center for Global Studies and the Humanities. His thinking concerns modernity/coloniality, geopolitics of knowledge, border thinking, pluriversality, and the decolonial option.

# Your Truths Are Self-Evident. Ours, a Mystery

By Basia Lewandowska Cummings
Monday, June 10, 2013

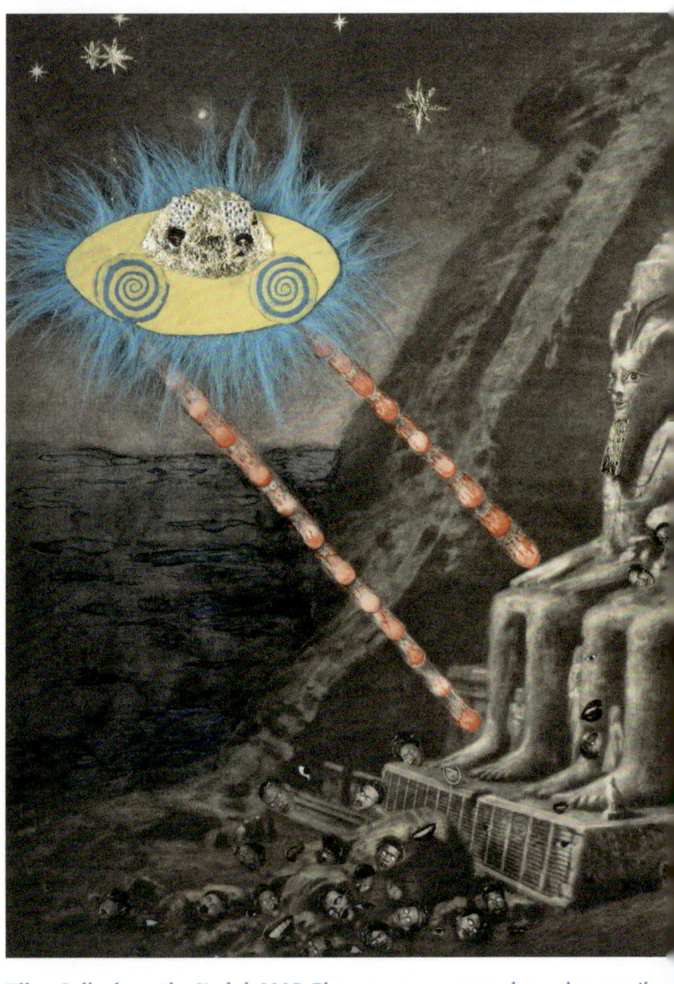

Ellen Gallagher, *Abu Simbel*, 2005. Photogravure, watercolor, color pencil, varnish, pomade, plasticine, blue fur, gold leaf, and crystals. Courtesy of the artist

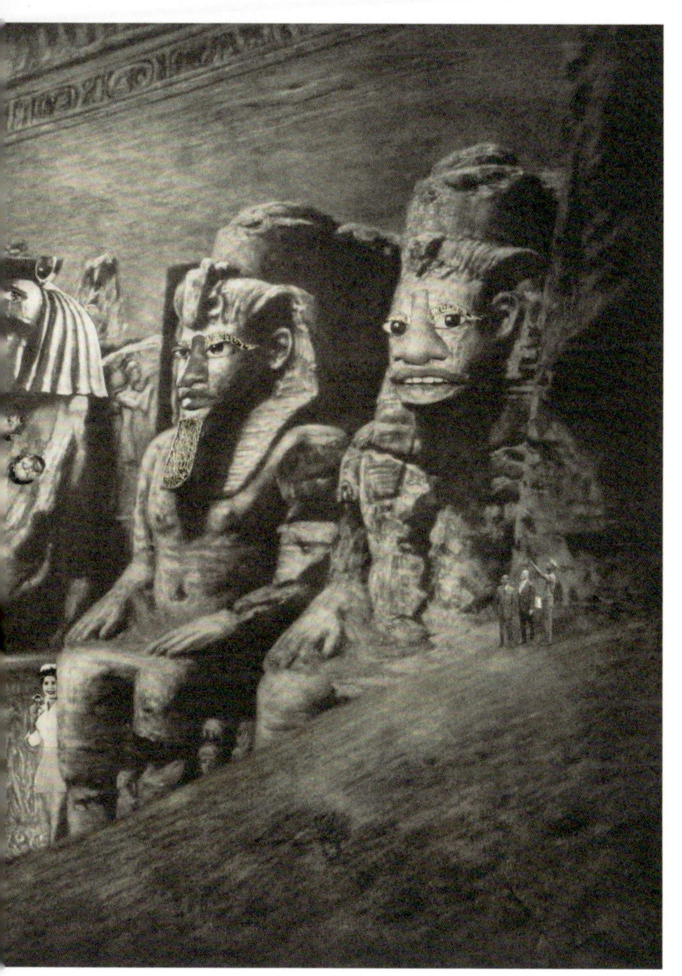

The English word "perspective" derives from the Latin, *perspectiva,* which means "to see through," and as such, instantly assumes a position—a viewer and a horizon, and an in-between space that demarcates self and other, subject and object, time and space. This is our modern perspective. Once this perspective is troubled—both visually and intellectually— orientation is challenged. As Hito Steyerl writes in her essay "In Free Fall"—"The horizon quivers in a maze of collapsing lines and you may lose any sense of above and below, or before and after, of yourself and your boundaries." But of course, in reality, these lines of sight (and thought) are always warped, tilted, troubled, and refracted, just as a horizon is seemingly stable, but exists in an infinite flux of relativity. To "see through," to gain perspective, or to "sight the object" is an illusion that the artist Ellen Gallagher relentlessly plays with. She challenges the relationship between visual perception and intellectual orientation, and in her work— which encompasses painting, sculpture, film, and collage—she defiantly challenges linear perspective to redress what fellow African-American artist Theaster Gates has called "the African non-archive."

A deep suspicion of linearity and its accompanying perspective (and indeed, the historical impulse behind it) is clearly felt in Gallagher's early work, where penmanship paper acts as the base upon which

169

she develops new symbolic vocabularies, riffing on
the repetitive early learning of written language.
But instead of practiced letters, Gallagher's papers
are inhabited by thousands of disembodied mouths
and ears, small, almost indistinguishable features
that dissolve into a rough geometry from afar. In
*Doll's Eyes* (1992), Gallagher's aesthetic recalls the
work of American minimalist Agnes Martin. But
Gallagher feels uneasy with this comparison, once
again preferring to align herself with a forgotten
Black history, in this case, with what she terms "the
earliest American abstraction" —minstrel shows
and the "disembodied ephemera of minstrelsy." In
*Purgatorium* (2000), Gallagher composes a vast grid
of thousands of hand-drawn mouths. She describes
how the paper plays tricks: "The lines of the penmanship paper sort of line up and, from a distance,
almost form a seamless kind of horizon line. But,
up close, you see that it's a kind of striated, broken
grid." Nothing is as it seems. Images shift and warp
according to how we position ourselves, both
physically and intellectually, in relation to her work,
perhaps a visual reflection of Stuart Hall's idea
that "identities are formed at the unstable point
where personal lives meet the narrative of history."

Ellen Gallagher's first retrospective in Great
Britain was at Tate Modern in 2013, featuring
around 100 works from 20 years. From the relative

calm of the watery-blue grids that line the opening room of "AxME" at Tate Modern, we moved through to the kaleidoscopic hot-box film installation *Osedax* (2009), witnessing as Gallagher jump cuts through cultural history, art history, oceanography, electronics, science fiction, and Detroit techno and back again. Her cultural references are frenetic. History is an arsenal to be mined and remixed, and her work, with all the wit and wildness she can muster, plugs the perceived voids and holes in the history of Black culture. The result is a startlingly complex web of narratives, a frenzy of interpretation where titles pun off everything and oblique references cut across works separated by decades, only to be summoned again two rooms later by the refrain of a disembodied mouth.

In *Murmur* (2003–04), a collaboration with Edgar Cleijne, a rattling projector illuminates a circular frame; plumes of steam, blue and diffuse, cut to images of animals bursting into light—combusting? Words appear on a black leader—"don't be afraid, it was in our power to"/"What happened?" but the significance of these words is dissolved by the inky light. Linguistic signs are meaningless here. A man stumbles, wearing some sort of burning yellow wig, distorted by the 16mm film stretch (an effect not dissimilar to wearing goggles under water). Gallagher is referencing the Drexciya myth, which imagines the children of pregnant slaves thrown overboard during the Middle Passage now existing as underwater creatures deep in the Atlantic Ocean. In turns, *Murmur* shifts between scenes appropriated and manipulated from old sci-fi films, to sequences from what look like old Westerns. Murmur dislodges time; an old future returns as a dark, watery myth reminding us of a horrific past. Gallagher has refracted history through the matter of its making; the ocean itself remoulds the form and the narrative.

This melting of subject and matter returns in the impressive two-part painting, *Bird in Hand* (2006) and *s'Odium* (2006), displayed here facing each other. A pirate, or slave trader, or Herman Melville's Captain Ahab—Gallagher is purposely oblique—stands underwater with a sprawling headpiece composed of warped faces (the cameos of drowned slaves?) and fragments of text extending outwards. He looks across at his dream, a vein-like plant pock-marked with gaps and holes recalling the eyes and mouths haunting Gallagher's earlier works. Again, layers of penmanship paper are used, but there is no longer a semblance of symmetry. Instead, pasted fluidly are archival maps, pages from beauty magazines and dissolving layers of watercolor. On the trader's body, Gallagher has attached shards of Himalayan rock salt, which shares the same mineral composition as the human body. An exchange of matter; an inscription of form into subject. A myth made plain. The work also draws on Gallagher's own history—her father was born in Cape Verde, a region which greatly prospered from salt mining, and for three hundred years functioned as the heart of the transatlantic slave trade.

But perhaps the most impressive of the works exhibited in "AxME" is the film installation *Osedax* (2009), another collaboration with Edgar Cleijne. Here, in a box, two walls are occupied by projections. In one of them, a slide projector beams kaleidoscopic images, etched and distorted by the artist's hand and magnified. Glass slides of alien life forms? The waterlogged kitenge fabric of African slaves, retrieved from the briny depths of the ocean? On the adjoining wall, a 16mm projector whirs, generating a heat which quickly becomes oppressive. In fact, the outside of the box is marked like a barnacle-encrusted whale skin—so are we inside the whale, looking out? In the film, an animated cormorant takes a dive, and a piece of music, sampled time and time again, hip-hop style, fills the gallery space. The box shifts from a whale's belly to a sweaty club. It's thrilling. The film cuts to an oil rig. Is it on fire? Are we actually in Sun Ra's spaceship, watching the demise of earth from afar? A shipwreck appears on screen, and in the spirit of the frenzy of association Gallagher has nurtured

throughout the exhibition, my exhausted mind
returns to Hito Steyerl's essay, to J. M. W. Turner's
*The Slave Ship* (1840)—a work that first disturbed
the horizon line in nautical painting—to slavery and
the Black Atlantic, to Géricault's *The Raft of the Medusa*
(1818–19), to Freud superimposed onto Matisse,
to Gallagher as the Odalisque, to Sun Ra's Dandies
and the golden circuit board …

It is endless.

A freefall of links, remixes, references and languages. Gallagher is relentless. But in her purposefully complex system of signs and references, the
artist goes a long way in achieving her aim, which is
to create a new Black history that is vivid, humorous,
defiant, militant, beautiful and impenetrable at
the same time.

As Sun Ra puts it, "Your truths are self-evident.
Ours, a mystery."

Basia Lewandowska Cummings is a London-based editor, writer, and
film curator. She writes for publications such as the *Guardian* and
*frieze* magazine.

# Does America Love Africa?

Cover headline, *Transition Magazine*, issue 25, 1966

# Will I Still Carry Water When I Am a Dead Woman?

*By Wana Udobang*
*Sunday, April 28, 2013*

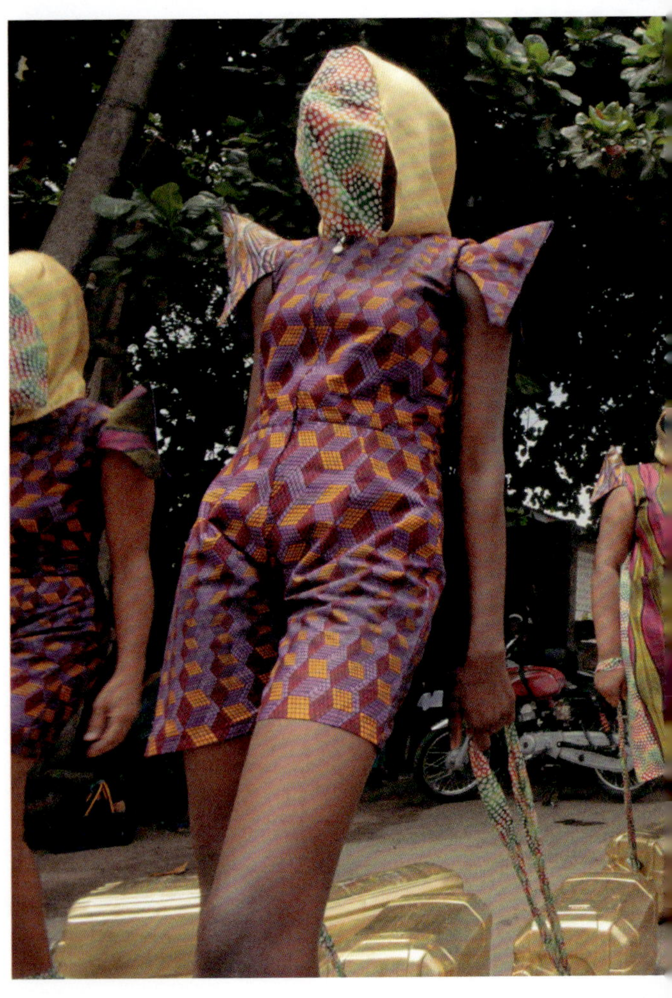

Wura-Natasha Ogunji, *Will I Still Carry Water When I Am a Dead Woman?*, 2013.
Performance in Lagos. Photo: Ema Edosio

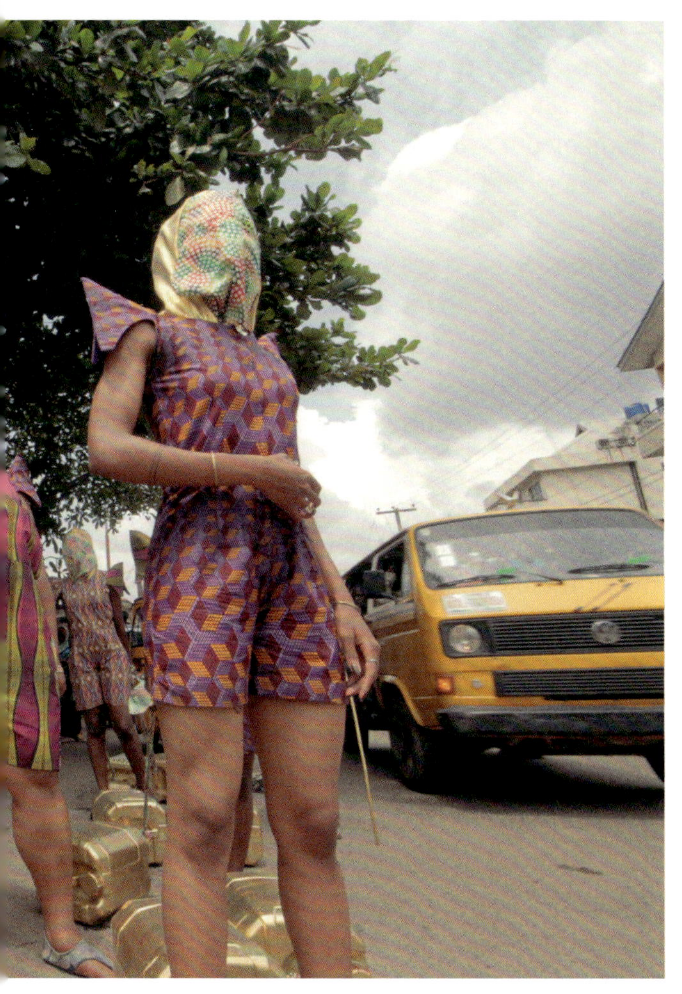

As far back as I can remember, I have always been an artist's guinea pig. Whether an extra in my friends Claire or Ghandi's student films or Victor Ehikhamenor's installation piece for his exhibition "Entrances and Exits," I am always a willing collaborator. This was the reason why when Nigerian/American artist Wura-Natasha Ogunji asked me to be a part of her performance piece titled *Will I Still Carry Water When I Am a Dead Woman?*, I couldn't refuse. The idea, she told me, would be this: myself and other women, dressed in mini-jumpsuits carrying kegs of water strapped to our ankles, would walk through the inner streets of Sabo, Yaba led by Ogunji herself and documented by videographer and filmmaker Ema Edosio. During hangouts with Ogunji, she had explained that she was very interested in using her work to explore women in public space. She had also mentioned her obsession with the Egungun masquerade and her curiosity as to why women were prohibited from the practice.

Our costumes were simultaneously an ode to and a rebellion against the Egungun, which Ogunji had termed the "futuristic Egungun." Perhaps it was our own way of rewriting the narrative of culture and history: wearing hooded mini-jumpsuits with pointed space like sleeves made from Ankara fabric with little holes punched through our masks to see through. Twenty-five-liter plastic kegs spray-painted

in gold and filled with water were strapped to each
ankle. I opted to drag mine with my hands due to
my already dodgy ankles. The journey started from
the Centre for Contemporary Arts (CCA) in Yaba
through the back roads of commercial avenue to the
final destination, which was Wura's house. I had
no expectations beyond the obvious gawking and
hurling of insults from bus conductors and puzzled
observers, however, the performance for me took
many different turns a little far off from what Ogunji
herself had anticipated. Mostly, these were anthropological and sociological in terms of participant
observation.

When we started, people looked, stared, and
some asked what we were doing. A gentleman even
went as far as dropping a hundred Naira note on my
shoulders. We dragged the kegs, leaving trails of
water behind. The friction between the plastic and
the tarred road had caused the containers to start
to give way. About twenty minutes into our roughly
two-mile journey, people stopped looking, stopped
caring, they just went about their business. Some of
us moved faster than the others, so at the beginning
we would stop and wait for the others to catch up.
Again, just as puzzled observers stopped observing,
we stopped waiting, and during the very few times
we did, I noticed the impatience and agitation in each
performer's body language, the sudden realization

that each woman had her own load to carry to the
finish point and thus the feeling of a certain lone-
liness through the journey.

The experience for me went beyond the test of
physical endurance, pain, rebellion, or even a loss
of self-awareness, but became more of a living and
breathing metaphor. Dragging the heavy containers
of water through public space became a symbol
of the expectations, desires, and roles society had
placed on women. More interesting was how
quickly the observers' curiosity diminished and the
realization that you had become the owner of the
burdens that have been placed on you. There was of
course the element of selfishness that brewed
among ourselves; you stopped waiting because you
became consumed with meeting the expectations
placed on you and getting to the finish line. At the
end of the journey, there was no victory parade,
no crowd cheering, no homecoming. One of Ogunji's
kegs had leaked through the journey and, at the
finish line, it was empty.

Wana Udobang is a multimedia journalist, writer, poet, and filmmaker, interested in the intersection between women's rights, personal
narratives, culture, and the arts.

We are the only
people who can get that
real spirit for us.

Charles Nkosi, artist

Editors

Julia Grosse is the co-founder and joint editor-in-chief of the art magazine *Contemporary And (C&)* focusing on African perspectives. She graduated in Art History, German Literature, and Media from Ruhr University Bochum, followed by working as a junior culture editor at Springer Verlag. Until 2013, Grosse worked as an arts correspondent in London for the *Frankfurter Allgemeine Sonntagszeitung*, *AD Magazine*, *SZ Magazin*, and *Tageszeitung*. In 2010 Grosse published *Don't Get Me Wrong!*, a handbook focusing on the many layers of global misunderstanding of hand gestures, which became a media hit and "book of the week" on CNN. She lives and works in Berlin.

Yvette Mutumba is the co-founder and joint editor-in-chief of the art magazine *Contemporary And (C&)*. She is a senior guest researcher of the project African Art History and the Formation of a Modern Aesthetic (2015–2018). From 2012 to 2016, she was a curator at Weltkulturen Museum in Frankfurt am Main, where she co-curated the major exhibitions "Foreign Exchange," "El Hadji Sy: Paintings, Performance, Politics," and "A Labour of Love," which was nominated for the 2016 Global Fine Arts Award. Mutumba studied Art History at Freie Universität, Berlin, and holds a PhD from Birkbeck, University of London. She has published numerous articles and books on contemporary art from African perspectives as well as global art history, and co-curated further projects on related topics. Recent publications include *A Labour of Love* (2015) and "Notes on Art and Food in Global Times" in *13th Fellbach Small Sculpture Triennial* (2016).

Elke aus dem Moore is Head of the Visual Arts Department at the Institute of Foreign Cultural Relations (ifa) in Stuttgart and Berlin, Germany. As a curator for contemporary art, she designs and initiates international exhibition programs that foster and focus on an exchange among artists from different societies while creating space for discussions of poltical and social issues. In this, she applies the same approach that characterized her tenures as curator at the Shedhalle in Zurich (1999–2002), and as artistic director of the Künstlerhaus Stuttgart (2003–2006). Elke aus dem Moore studied literature and art history in Osnabrück, Zürich, and Bochum. She is responsible for an international exhibition program, conferences on biennial culture, online magazines, and funding programs. Some of the major projects she established are "Pret-a-Partager," an artistic platform in several African cities and the *Contemporary And*. Recent projects are "Future Memories" (2015), a conference in Addis Abeba and an online platform on art in public space, and the research and exhibition project "Politics of Sharing: On Collective Wisdom" in (2016–17).

Edited by ifa (Elke aus dem Moore)
and C& (Julia Grosse and Yvette Mutumba)

Copy editing: Jenifer Evans, Jake Schneider, Ekpenyong Ani
Design: Studio Matthias Görlich
Typeface: Rosart (Camelot Typefaces)
Image Credits: © authors, photographers, artists

Anthology © 2017, Berlin

Published by Sternberg Press

Printed in Germany
ISBN 978-3-956793-29-5

Thank you to all the contributors.
www.contemporaryand.com

Sternberg Press
Caroline Schneider
Karl-Marx-Allee 78
D-10243 Berlin
www.sternberg-press.com

Federal Foreign Office